The Day of the Dead

F. Gonzalez-Crussi

The Day of the Dead
And Other Mortal Reflections

A Harvest Book
Harcourt Brace & Company
San Diego   New York   London

Requests for permission to make copies
of any part of the work should be mailed to:
Permissions Department, Harcourt Brace & Company,
6277 Sea Harbor Drive, Orlando, Florida 32887-6777.

The essay "Two Unrecorded Scenes" previously
appeared in *The New Yorker*.

Library of Congress Cataloging-in-Publication Data
Gonzalez-Crussi, F.
The day of the dead: and other mortal reflections/F. Gonzalez-Crussi.
        p.   cm. — (A Harvest book)
Originally published: New York: Harcourt Brace and Co., 1993.
Includes bibliographical references.
ISBN 0-15-600142-X
1. Death. 2. Autopsy. 3. Death in art. 4. Embalming.   I. Title.
[R726.8.G68   1994]
616.07'8 — dc20   94-3409

Designed by Camilla Filancia
Printed in the United States of America
First Harvest edition 1994   A B C D E

Contents

Preface

In the fall of 1991, the British Broadcasting Corporation (BBC) first proposed that I collaborate in a documentary film for a television series entitled "Bookmark," which reviews the work of writers and attempts to portray the varied conditions under which the highly private and all too often Sisyphean writing task continues to be stubbornly cultivated today. Mr. Kevin Hull, the young and talented director who contacted me, was aware of my identity as a medical man, a pathologist. I suppose he wished to show that the highly technological setting of a pathology laboratory is not incompatible with a purely literary ministry. Predictably, after the director watched an autopsy, the powerful spectacle of death and dissection dominated all else. The documentary became not so much a filmic exploration of the improbable links between literature and a modern medical discipline as a stark visual record of mortality. With filmmaking crews we visited cemeteries in two countries, shot scenes of dying patients, interviewed embalmers, recorded burials, and paced, undaunted, the gloomy haunts of coroners, undertakers, and morgue attendants.

The final product was aired on public television in England (BBC2) late at night on April 27, 1992, when children were reasonably expected to be in bed.

The idea to write this book emerged during the filming process. Word and image do not compete with each other: each thrives in its own domain. Accordingly, the present book is not "based" on the documentary. It is not a description of the film, but an attempt to cast into literary form the varied reflections or meditations sparked along the way and the experiences incurred, often behind the cameras, in the course of the production.

The Day of the Dead

A Visit to the Embalmer

A letter informs me that the prestigious British Broadcasting Corporation (BBC) is interested in producing a documentary film for television, based largely upon my writings. Such news awakens brisk feelings, not wholly of a positive character. To be sure, I feel flattered that my work should have attracted the attention of important opinion makers. But I am also leery of the tenor of the anticipated film. For the documentary's central theme, it is announced, will be death. This means I ·have been singled out as a writer preoccupied with depressing topics: a mortuary pen, as it were. Such is the sad condition of my originality and the source of my wariness. Many writers are also lawyers, anthropologists, or college professors: a few, physicians. A noted novelist is also a priest. None, as far as I know, are corpse handlers; none hold as intimate a commerce with the dead as I do. I suspect this unique circumstance must have weighed in the public's favor, always with a bent for the bizarre.

Hence, my confusion and bewilderment. Demosthenes heard his critics say that his speeches smelled of the lamp's oil—a sarcastic allusion to his long overnight vigils preparing every word of his orations, which turned out supremely elegant but wanting in freshness and spontaneity. "Your lamp and mine," he is reported to have answered, "are not conscious of the same things." But what if my own productions were said to reek of decomposing flesh? I would be at a loss seeking the tit for tat. Genial satiric wits could counterattack by dipping their pens in acid, or in poison, as the trite metaphor says. What would I dip mine into? Blood effusions? Ascitic fluid? Cadaveric serosities?

Before long, the film producer appears. Never having met one before, I can only wonder whether his black pullover and black suit are customary attire in filmic circles, or are part of a calculated, subtle strategy: the garb of an aspiring explorer of the netherworld whose forethought prepared the colors of mourning. We talk about the discipline of pathology, its place in medicine, its glorious past, and its present quandaries. We visit the various sections of the laboratory where I work. But the conversation returns, predictably, to death, the autopsy, and the study of cadavers. The suggestion, formerly put forth in summary fashion, of visiting an embalmer's outfit, is now reiterated more forcefully. I protest that I know no more about this profession than any other person, that my previous writings bearing on this activity were based on bibliographic research, not firsthand observations. At the same time, however, I say to myself that perhaps I have been remiss in my duties. Truly conscientious workers never rest content within the narrow circle of their routines. Pathologist and embalmer, though diverging in interests, have reasons to fraternize. Both find themselves unwitting trespassers in the realm of the sacred, since both confront the dead and the body's interior. On a practical level, these two workers are in a position to influence each other's business, as those would readily agree who are familiar with the day-to-day practice of the respective occupations. In sum, I agree that the projected visit would not be a loss of time and might even cast a new and unsuspected light, however peripheral, upon my own activities. As it turns out, Miss X, who holds the job of morgue attendant at my place of work, is a licensed embalmer and has the right connections. The three of us make for a funeral home in a blue-collar neighborhood of West Chicago.

"Funeral home," with the emphasis on "home," is but one example of the universal obliquity of death-related discourse. If it is true that words are not merely the dress of thought, but, as Merleau-Ponty believed, "its very flesh and substance," then the word *death* is an exception. It could not be otherwise, since death is essentially uncontemplable, unthinkable, and beyond all possibility of description. Therefore it must elude discourse; and the tendency to evade naming this reality must be universal. The dead have not died, but "passed on," "ceased to be," or simply "left us." They were removed from earthly concerns in ways that range from exalted—"called away by our Maker"—to neutral or indifferent—"rests in peace"—but are almost always dignified. Slang replaces dignity with various forms of abuse: "kicked the bucket," "croaked," and so on. But even those who would scoff with abusive or facetious language have only to be faced with the spectacle of their beloved dead— their mother, father, spouse, or dearest friend—for their mockeries instantly to cease. Scorn then turns to sadness, and acid wit to piteous sorrow. The former scoffers will go to great lengths to recuperate the mortal remains of their loved ones; pay high sums to ensure shipments across continents or provide for elaborate ceremonies; preserve as objects of veneration and worship a few bones, a heap of ashes: the same things that minutes before were casually held up to public ridicule. Mark the venomous lampooner: his barb now blunted, he consigns the cherished remains to a cemetery (from the Greek *koimeterion,* "a place to sleep") and engraves on stone such solemn phrases as "here rests in peace . . ."—but there is no sleeping or resting peaceably here: only decay.

The same proclivity for denial or avoidance has baptized the place we visit with the name "funeral home." "Funerarium," once in use, was soon discarded as too esoteric, foreign, and raising unwanted associations of ideas. "Home" is the name dearest, by no coincidence, to funeral directors and real estate agents alike. It evokes scenes of quiet domestic peace; of a fire crackling on the hearth; of the family gathered in a circle, such as Greuze, Chardin, or Norman Rockwell might have painted. The sign is conspicuous. The entrance is covered by a blue-and-white awning that extends to the curbside.

The moment we cross the threshold, an odd feeling seizes us. Stimulation of the sensorium is suddenly reduced to a minimum. Sounds are muffled by insulated walls. Colors, modulated to low levels of warmth, blend and harmonize in a soothing manner. Thick carpets in sober colors, heavy draperies, mahogany sideboards, and diffused lights

accentuate the aura of quiet collectedness.
The ceilings are very high. An ornate crystal
chandelier, complemented by light fixtures
shaped as burning candles on the lateral
walls, spreads a soft light that can be pro-
gressively dimmed by rotary switches. It is a
place of solemnity, divorced from the tumult
of the street. Automatically, we lower our
voices, conscious of finding ourselves in a
place that was brought into form for the purpose of venting grief and exchanging con-
dolences. "Differentiated" space.

It is a commonplace that in the United
States the "funeral industry" has flourished
into a billion-dollar business plagued by
abuses and outrageous misconduct. The lu-
dicrous and reprehensible incidents stem-
ming from a desire for profit have occupied
me and many others elsewhere. Today, I am
here on a social call, utterly unsolicited. Mr.
J., our host, is most gracious. For reasons that
escape me, my BBC friend finds the scene
"Pathologist Meets Embalmer," as he calls
it, eminently cinematic. He regrets not having
cameras on hand to capture it in all its
spontaneity.

Mr. J. shows us the administrative offices, the parlors, the family room, and chapels A and B, divided by a foldable partition that allows their mutual merging into a larger enclosure fit to accommodate a great number of people in crowded funeral ceremonies. Each chapel has a lectern, rows of seats with velvet upholstery, a crucifix in Flemish bronze, lamps supported by sculpted columns, medallions on the walls, and large floral displays. Gold-laminated or Bakelite signs with black or white lettering mark the various areas. The focal point is the showroom, where the caskets are displayed. They are exhibited on elegant supports, under careful lighting conditions that enhance their attractiveness. For a thing of beauty they are, indeed. Let the skeptical philosopher inveigh against the futility of the effort behind the superb craftsmanship; and let his dyspeptic followers rail against the uselessness, the vanity of shaping these beautiful vessels that are to crumble, unseen, carrying their putrefying cargo to the bowels of the earth. The fact remains that they are beautiful: oak, solid mahogany, stainless steel, polystyrene, sculpted elaborately or smoothed to a glossy finish, with handmade interiors of satin or velvet, ceramic appliqués, embossed doeskin coverings—in a word, conveyances to fit all sizes, tastes, and purses.

A corridor leads to a room that our host refers to matter-of-factly as "the operating room." But we are not going there now. Instead, we climb upstairs, to the living quarters of Mr. and Mrs. J. A detail delights my filmic friend as we climb the stairs: the drapes that cover a window are actually a stitched casket lining in soft pastel blue. It fits to perfection.

I had expected a sharp contrast between the upstairs and the downstairs; between the accommodations of the living and the lodgings of the dead. I am amazed to find that no trenchant disparity exists. The old couple in charge of the funeral home have managed to impart the same subdued, mellow atmosphere to the entire building. It is a house from which strong sensations are barred: bright colors obtrude nowhere, and sharp sounds will not trouble the calm, toneless ambience. I regret lacking the unhurried and compulsive descriptive powers of a Marcel

Proust, for the scene before my eyes ought to be framed in the most meticulous and prolix of styles. Plodding language of fastidious turns could alone do justice to the crowded daintiness, the gimcrackery bathed in silence that is here displayed. Alternatively, cause and effect may be imagined reversed. A Proustian style must spring from such a place: it must be the natural efflorescence of a boy's mind developing under the tutelage of a grandmother, or an old aunt, in a room like this.

Despite the pervading torpor, and a stubborn sensation, which is odorless, but which I can describe no better than with the word *mustiness*, it would be untrue, and manifestly unfair, to say that the upstairs ambience is funereal. The sense of stagnation and moldiness is undone by the vitality of our hosts. Mr. and Mrs. J. are attentive, sensible, and warmly communicative. Mr. J., though very advanced in years, is alert, eloquent, witty, and entertaining. Sixty years in the business! A repository of anecdotes and matchless embalming experience, this rosy-cheeked, white-haired gentleman exudes sympathy. A real gem.

We settle, over coffee, to animated conversation. Much to the filmmaker's enjoyment, the initial discussion focuses on the relation between pathologist and embalmer. The latter's job begins, ordinarily, when the former's has ended. "We ought to talk more often," says Mr. J. at one point, and I can only agree. But soon the conversation turns to various aspects of his trade. We ask him to reminisce on noteworthy cases of his experience. His career, he tells us, started in the thirties. One of the most notable cases he recollects was that of the Chicago gangster, John Dillinger. He did not perform the embalming of the notorious personage, but he was acquainted with those who did, and, in a manner of speaking, an apprentice of the same. Mr. J. needs no prompting to embark on the narrative that follows, punctuated with explanatory digressions for the benefit of the foreign visitor.

On a fateful evening in July 1934, the famous gangster John Dillinger was lured by a mysterious "woman in red" from the ticket window of the Biograph Theater, a popular movie house on Chicago's Lincoln Avenue, to a deserted alley close by. An ambush had been carefully laid for the purpose of ending, once and for all, the malefactor's career. Plainclothesmen were positioned at strategic sites, while other policemen disguised as city workers had placed signs to divert the incoming traffic. No sooner did Dillinger tread on a previously designated place than a veritable hail of automatic gunfire rained upon him from rooftops, ledges, building corners, and the most unlikely hideouts. The Public Enemy Number One, robber of banks in multiple states of the Union, and slayer of guardians of the public order, fell with a heavy, dry thump, his corpulent frame sprawling on the alley's dusty ground, never to rise again.

That criminals who target the rich earn the affection of the dispossessed is no secret. This is especially so in bleak times. The acute misery of the poor finds uncharitable solace in the visible distress of those who, obscurely and intuitively, are held accountable for their poverty. The popular masses, still smarting from the furious lashes of the Great Depression, looked in consternation upon the fallen gangster. A legend then originated, which is yet to die more than a half century later.

"Dillinger Alley" is the name that oral tradition, if not the official city maps, confers to the squalid place. The neighbors can still watch today the regular visit of a tourist enterprise, Untouchable Tours, which ferries groups of visitors on black-painted buses, while guides in the garb of gangsters of yore—Panama hat, black shirt, white necktie, striped suit, and a holster with a realistic toy gun at axillary level, under the jacket—briefly describe the nefarious occurrence, then take off to extol one or another of the many "glories" that grace the history of the Windy City.

Unbecoming as this popular homage may seem, it is as nothing compared to the outpouring of sympathy that took place in the summer of 1934. Throngs gazed into the lifeless, opaque eyes of their infamous idol. The police were unable to restrain the crowd's morbid curiosity. Women dipped handkerchiefs in the blood of the felon, not unlike fervent royalists in France, centuries earlier, who had vied with each other to dip lace and silks in the blood of their beheaded monarchs, braving the risks of the Terror.

Scavengers chipped off pieces of the wooden post on which Dillinger's blood had splattered and took them to all points of the nation, just as relics of saints were dispersed to all parts of Christendom by the zeal of the faithful. The post was so badly chiseled and scalloped that the electric company had to be called in to replace it. The body was transported to the Alexian Brothers Hospital. Crowds followed, before which, according to my informant, the slain gangster continued to pose as benefactor. Seeing that the crowd's curiosity did not abate, two morgue attendants contrived to place the corpse on a stretcher, elevated on an incline so that the face would be clearly visible from an opening in the door, and managed to organize the pressing multitude into a moving row of watchers who peeped through the postern— for a dime apiece—then moved on promptly at the urgings of the attendants.

These carryings-on continued through the night. At length, the regular medical staff in charge of the morgue came by and did not take kindly to the idea of an evildoer lying in state, as if he were a national hero, or to the mercenary method of his exhibition. The ongoing proceedings were rudely interrupted. What those in authority did not know is that the resourceful morgue attendants had managed to produce one or more postmortem facial imprints of the slain criminal. One of these was smuggled out of the morgue, with the idea, no doubt, of mass-producing the likeness of the now legendary outlaw for a profit. The business did not come to fruition. Word reached the FBI that the mold existed, and the attendant who had it was startled one night, when special agents loudly rapped at his door. The cast was requisitioned, on the premise that it constituted valuable evidence for the trials and investigations that followed the slaying. Many years later the coveted object ended up in the possession of a Mr. Crewdson, noted criminologist, who sold it to an antiquarian.

Mr. J. ended his narrative by showing us a printed catalogue of a Chicago auctioneer, in which a death mask of John Dillinger is reproduced. A caption indicates that it was sold in September of 1991 for ten thousand dollars. The purchaser's name was undisclosed, but, added our informant with a twinkle in his eye, was known to be an Englishman.

Mr. J.'s narrative makes me reflect on the forces that may have actuated the morgue attendants. To make an image of the deceased is a very ancient custom, but to obtain a facial imprint by means of wax or other suitable materials seems to carry special and subtle meanings. It seems different from attempting to reproduce the likeness of a dead person in a painting, or in sculpture. When wax or a malleable substance is used, the impression is obtained by intimate contact between the moldable material and the object reproduced. There is no space, no discontinuity between the two. In a certain sense it may be said that the wax becomes, during the imprinting, a physical extension of the dead person's face; and therefore the wax imprint is thought to contain an element of the objective reality of the model that a sculpture or a painting cannot seize. No form of copy, regardless of how skillful the artist who attempts it, will ever grasp this reality. For a sculpture or a painting will always contain something of the artist's personality, which is why an artistic production is called a "creation." Artistic work must be imbued with elements of the creator's sensibility, fancy, and so on. But between face and mask-imprint, nothing is interposed. Modern photography, being two-dimensional, also falls short of the power of the wax impression, which brings back something of the physical presence of the departed into the world of the living. This something is neither the soul, which is ethereal and indivisible, nor a part of the body, which is now lifeless. It is what the ancient Greeks might have called "form," an element of the physical quality of the body that detaches itself, uncorrupted, from the dead remains. Wondrous to remark, this ineffable principle retains the suggestive powers of the soul and the reproductive capacity of the body, since out of a mold an infinite series of masks—each an identical immanent presence—may be fashioned.

The ongoing conversation brings me back from these idle musings. Mr. J. has modestly asserted that although he has personally embalmed nearly two thousand cadavers, none was as famous as Dillinger's. His shop sits in a section of the city that is strictly lower middle class. Through his hands have passed aldermen, union organizers, and sundry community leaders, but none was a national figure. The neighborhood seems such that a person rising to national prominence would be expected to move out. And whereas nostalgia is known to dictate testaments that specify a posthumous return to the native ground, seldom is the last will sufficiently explicit to comprehend the services of the neighborhood's embalmer.

On the other hand, the quiet discharge of one's duties is ever preferable to the bustle and agitation of fame. This maxim, self-evident in the transactions of the living, applies equally well after the body has perished. Mr. J. knows this very well, for he has studied with a discerning eye the vicissitudes of famous dead bodies that were rendered nearly indestructible through his art. He has published in journals of his trade an account of the tribulations of the postmortem career of Eva ("Evita") Perón, the renowned though unofficial Argentinian leader. His chronicle seemed to me sufficiently engrossing to be worth retelling here, with full acknowledgment of my only source.[1]

Eva Ibarguren Duarte Perón, popularly known as Evita, was an aspiring young actress in Buenos Aires in the early 1940s. She suffered the many frustrations that stand in the way of those who hanker after public applause. For years she had only minor roles in films and on radio, but her luck changed dramatically in 1945, when she married Juan Domingo Perón (1895–1974), then vice president and minister of war. Juan had participated in the 1943 *coup d'état* by which a military junta (he was then army colonel) seized power. Evita became a populist in the most baroque and elaborate sense of the word; some say a demagogue to match the most sophisticated world leaders worthy of this name. She attained marked visibility in the public life of her country. She was regarded, as the *Encyclopedia Britannica* puts it, "de facto minister of health and of labour." She founded orphanages, nursing schools, and philanthropic associations; inaugurated hospitals and medical institutes;

fought with success for the suffrage of women; secured low-cost housing, better wages, and good retirement pensions for workers; and by various showy manifestations of concern for the common weal endeared herself to the masses. Together with this enlightened largesse she managed to amass an enormous personal fortune. Her jewelry was valued at about ten million dollars. It included the extraordinary collar of San Martin, an Argentinian decoration ornamented with 753 precious stones in all, held by gold and platinum chains of staggering cost. Her personal wardrobe, supplied by a Paris couturier known to have collected from her over forty thousand dollars in a year, was stocked with forty superb mink coats, an ermine cape, and endless items of stylish and costly apparel. This conspicuous consumption was punctually defrayed by disbursements from Swiss bank accounts, but ultimately came from the taxation levied on the Argentinian people, an important segment of which would have preferred different "allocation of resources," as they say in bureaucratic circles.

Little avails the power and the pride before the Great Leveler. She was mortal, like the rest of us. The most famous medical specialists could do nothing to stave off the cancer that consumed her. The beautiful young woman shrank to an emaciated shadow of her former self; she weighed a mere sixty-five pounds the day she died, July 26, 1952.

Enter the embalmer. Dr. Pedro Ara (1891–1973), a native of Zaragoza, Spain, had achieved some notoriety as an expert in the preparation of cadavers for anatomical dissection and was recommended to Perón through connections he acquired in his capacity as cultural attaché of the Spanish embassy in Buenos Aires. Perón had decided, as soon as it was clear that the demise of his wife was imminent, that her remains would be enshrined in a superb monument and exposed to the adoring masses. As the remains of Lenin were a source of ever-renewing ideological fervor for communists, so would Evita's fuel the unflagging popular enthusiasm for the social and economic conquests of Peronismo. Guards were posted at the door of the room of the presidential palace where Dr.

Ara, working through the night, performed his ministrations. No one, not even the supreme Chief of State, could enter without the explicit permission of the physician-embalmer. What Dr. Ara did is a matter of no small import to those of the trade. Mr. J., from whose written narrative these facts are extracted, believes it was intra-arterial injection of paraffin and formalin, followed by total immersion of the body in a tank of liquid paraffin. There is cause to regret that Dr. Ara was secretive about his methods, which were described all too succinctly in a publication now out of print, in Spanish, and with a most distressing paucity of details.

Be that as it may, when Dr. Ara's work was done, Evita's body was cleansed, her hair arranged, and her delicate frame clad in an elegant white robe. A distressed President Perón contemplated the body of his dead wife after it was placed in a glass-lidded mahogany coffin. In her hands was the mother-of-pearl rosary that she once received from the Pope, and on her chest the exquisitely wrought golden emblem of the Peronista party, enchased with precious stones. He asked the embalmer how long her remains would stand without decomposition. Dr. Ara replied, with a cockiness in which the better part of prudence made way for professional pride: "Forever."

Now the nation surrendered to boundless, uncontrollable grief. Buildings were draped in black, flags flew at half-mast, public services were interrupted for several days, and literally millions of Argentinians wearing black armbands paraded in front of Evita's coffined remains during the weeks when these were laid in state at the Ministry of Labor. On August ninth, a solemn, magnificent funeral procession carried the body through the streets of Buenos Aires to the National Labor Union Headquarters, known as the CGT, where Dr. Ara performed additional manipulations. These presumably consisted of further intra-arterial injections of formalin, glycerine, alcohol, and thymol. His solicitude was amply rewarded. The fee paid for his services is not known, but at one time the accusation was leveled at him by impugners of having collected over 300,000 U.S. dollars. Dr. Ara claimed to have received less than 50,000 dollars all told, a fee that might be esteemed high even in the most select circles of the American Funeral Directors Association.

Politics, it hardly needs reiteration, is an ungrateful and often seedy affair. As the fortunes of Peronismo vacillated, all who had associated with the regime came under suspicion and criticism. Caught in the vortex of clashing factional rancors, Dr. Ara, too, was suspected of wrongdoing. But how is an embalmer to cheat when his handiwork remains under constant view, exhibited before the eyes of millions? The accusations against him have the flavor of the extravagances of Latin American novelists of the magical-realist persuasion. They were, nonetheless, made in earnest, and so propounded as to annex a considerable number of believers. At one time or another the following rumors spread throughout the nation: that the cadaver exhibited at the CGT headquarters was not a human corpse, but a mannequin or wax statue; that it was a composite fashioned out of Eva Perón's head and an artificial, incorruptible body, or someone else's body, a kind of postmortem chimera; or that the cadaver was not Eva Perón's, but that of another female of similar physique, cleverly contrived by reconstructive surgery to simulate the likeness of the true Evita.

For Evita, or what remained of her, this was only the beginning of her post-death tribulations. In 1955 the Perón regime came to an abrupt end, via the obligatory "coup." Perón went into exile. The new president, Colonel Pedro Aramburu (1903–1970), was quick to realize that his power would never be consolidated so long as there existed a symbol for his enemies to rally around. This symbol, constantly infusing his foes with zeal for their inimical credo, was Evita's body. Alas, that symbol had been prepared to last "forever." Dr. Ara, of course, was not about to forswear his original boast. There is, after all, such a thing as a hypertrophic concept of honor among Spaniards. This national peculiarity now led him to embellish his claim. Evita's body, he said, could not be undone by time, ruined by moldy growths, corrupted by bacteria, or any other natural agents. In fact, he said, now somewhat piqued, it would resist immersion in strong acids and would in all likelihood emerge intact from fire.

Perhaps these exaggerated claims contributed to the imaginative plans of the officers of the new junta to rid the country, and the planet, of the stubborn presence. They considered dropping the body into the crater of a smoldering volcano, or from an airplane into the high seas, or burying it under an airstrip in a remote island of Argentina's South Arctic possessions. Perón foiled these projects with his own plan, a cloak-and-dagger scheme worthy of a mystery novel. The body was to be kidnapped. It was to be abducted under the very nose of its guardians by special commandos. The daring group was apparently under the direction of a world-renowned German military officer, Otto Skórzeny. This man had engineered the bold rescue of Benito Mussolini from a European mountaintop resort.*

By whatever means it was carried out, the abduction of Evita's body was flawlessly executed. Evita's post-death vicissitudes

---

* The Argentinian government had sympathized with the Nazis during the second World War, and Skórzeny, like other German military, had found an asylum in South America. It was rumored that his connections with influential persons of the Perón regime allowed him to implement a major plan, the "Odessa Operation," that rendered possible the evasion of German officers from the avenging arm of their unforgiving vanquishers.

were under way. It seems that she was kept for a while in a secret room of the military intelligence headquarters by loyal Peronistas. An officer was entrusted with her custody. Apprehensive over the momentous importance of his charge, he is said to have slept in the same room with the coffin and its contents, and to have kept a loaded gun under his pillow. The unverified story adds that, waking up one time in the middle of the night, sweaty and frightened, he lethally shot his pregnant wife, by mistake.

The Peronistas could not have kept the body indefinitely. This is why they crated it and shipped it out of the country; in one version, to the Argentinian embassy in Bonn, Germany, unbeknownst to the official ambassador. From here, the body found its way to Italy, always with the cooperation of high government officials along the way and in the various countries concerned in the transfer. Evita was buried under the assumed identity of a Maria Maggi, Italian immigrant to Argentina, in a Milanese cemetery in 1957, perhaps after a temporary residence in another cemetery in Rome.

Meanwhile, the worst fears of the new Argentinian government became a reality. The Peronistas still clamored for the return of their former leader, and surreptitiously agitated. They rallied around the always viable symbol, the dead body of Evita. Signs declaring Where is Evita's Body? and Return Our Lady to Us appeared mysteriously on walls, while a murderous guerrilla war raged throughout the country. Aramburu was no longer president. Unfortunately, while in power he had imprudently boasted of knowing where Evita's body was. Guerrillas kidnapped him, and tortured him, presumably to force him to disclose the secret. Aramburu died under torture.

These ominous developments prompted Juan Domingo Perón, now in exile, to retrieve the body of his dead wife. Indeed, whichever party won in the struggle, the consequences were equally unseemly for Evita. If the new Argentinian government really knew her whereabouts, it was not inconceivable that an effort might be made to disinter her and destroy her, thus putting an end to her pernicious postmortem activities as *agente pro-*

vocatrice. But if the rebels were victorious, they could also adduce reasons to wish to appropriate Evita's body and use it as a symbol for their cause, always in a way most hurtful to Perón's sensibility and without his acquiescence.

Therefore, by means that are not altogether clear, but in which many see again the shady intervention of Otto Skórzeny, the body was exhumed and transported to Madrid. It should be noted that three important personages, Dr. Pedro Ara, Otto Skórzeny, and Juan Domingo Perón, were living in quiet retirement in Madrid. The three of them must have watched with bated breath one day the opening of the deteriorated coffin. Nor is it unwarranted to state that Ara's was the greatest thrill in this occasion. Nineteen years after the embalming, he could still claim that his boast had not been vain. Hardly a mark of damage marred his work: a bent ear here, a broken finger there, caused by previous efforts at obtaining fingerprints for identification. Minor repairs were all that was needed.

Evita's remains were restored, dressed in new clothes, and placed in a new coffin. She was installed in a new room of the second floor of Perón's Madrid home. He was now living with his third wife, but this detail seems not to have interfered with an easy transition into a *ménage à trois*, or perhaps more appropriately, *à deux et demie*. The evening meal was taken by the married couple in the same room where Evita reposed.

The story closes with one more tempestuous episode. The political seesaw again inclined in favor of Perón. He returned to Argentina, and to power, in 1973, accompanied by his third wife. A year later he died suddenly, apparently of a heart attack. It was appointed that his wife would succeed him in the presidency. However, Peronismo had a new face: those who had idolized the charismatic Evita felt no attachment to her successor. Unruly mobs broke into the Recoleta cemetery and dug out the remains of former president Aramburu, whom many still held responsible for the unjust banishment of Evita's presence from the fatherland. Who said human beings are merely passive agents after the body has perished? A dead ex-president

Aramburu was held ransom until the equally dead Evita would be returned. Such was the clear condition of the rebels. The surviving widow had no option but to order the return of her predeceased predecessor. The body arrived in early December of 1974 and was deposed in a crypt by the side of Juan Domingo Perón. Two years later they were separated again, transferred to their respective family entombments.

Mr. J.'s article, whose main points it has been my pleasure to retell here, ends on a note of understandable professional pride. It notes that, as the two coffins lay side by side, Juan's was closed, and Evita's open. Sure mark, writes Mr. J., that the former's body had succumbed to the ravages of postmortem decay, whereas Evita, having been under the able superintendence of a member of the embalmers' profession, looked as fresh twenty years after her death as if she had fallen asleep just the night before.

Before leaving the premises we are conducted to Mr. J.'s "operating room." It is downstairs, by the garage. The cadaver of a young man is there, looking, indeed, as if asleep. A worthy sample to show to visitors! Miss X, our companion, was to comment later on the inconveniences of funeral home franchising. Funeral homes apparently offer good wages and free housing to qualified, licensed embalmers. The trouble is, it is necessary to resign oneself to sharing the comfortable home with downstairs tenants, albeit remarkably quiet ones. "My family would never come to visit me," says our companion with regret. We all assent. It is not by coincidence that the magazines of the embalmer's trade include frequent stories of ghosts and apparitions. Mr. J. answers all our queries, expounding with gusto on the many technical details of his art. He reminisces about the early era of his practice when embalmers were divided by petty and invidious concerns—for rancor and dissension may be found, it seems, in every human group. At that time, he says, those who practiced intra-arterial embalming referred to those who punctured the abdomen as "belly punchers," since they used a coarse method of embalming requiring no knowledge of anatomy. The slighted ones countered by nicknaming their disdainers "throat slashers," an unfair and inaccurate label, since no further incisions are required to inject the carotid arteries after an autopsy has been completed.

The hour is late, and we must take our leave. We thank our gracious hosts for their most instructive cooperation and generous courtesy. Mr. J. sees us to the door, always as charming and full of octogenarian joviality as at the beginning of our visit. We exit from the murk and sensory dimness of his establishment into the open air. The brisk, vivifying autumnal air hits me on the face, as I think of one of Pascal's remarks in his *Pensées*: "Death is easier to endure if you don't think about it, than is the thought of death when there is no danger of it." And Voltaire's rebuttal, in one of his letters: "It cannot be said that a man endures death easily or uneasily when he does not think about it at all. He who feels nothing endures nothing."[2]

The Grin of the *Calavera*

The decision has been made that some of the film sequences will be shot in Mexico. For a film centered on the idea of death, this choice makes eminently good sense. The world is aware that on the first two days of November, which the Catholic ritual calendar reserves to remember the departed of the family, Mexico embarks on a national celebration marked by a tone of ebullient festivity that usually astounds, and sometimes shocks, the unprepared visitor. November is almost here, and there is just enough time to make our travel arrangements.

Days later, from the window of an air-craft, I catch sight of the huge, sprawling metropolis. Mexico City! In adamantine prose, Alfonso Reyes, peerless master of Spanish letters, once called the valley of Mexico "the most transparent region of the air." A quick glance from my observation post quickly dispels the illusion in the poetical conceit. A thick cloud of toxic fumes hangs over the entire city, traversed by the waves of local broadcasts that warn of the dangers of the atmospheric levels of ozone. Over twenty million people, close to one third of the entire population of the country, form the vibrant, teeming, cruel, tender, affable, and desperate mass of humanity before my eyes. The metropolitan area is known by the abbreviation D.F., for *Distrito Federal*. With a touch of that cruel humor that characterizes the natives, they are prompt to point out that the initials really stand for *Defiéndete*—"Defend yourself."

On the way to the hotel I ask myself whether the same forces that rendered Alfonso Reyes's lyrical outburst obsolete and fallacious might not have also altered in similar fashion the festivities we came to watch, namely the celebration of *El Día de los Muertos*, or "the Day of the Dead," for such is the popular local style of reference to All Saints' Day. There are disquieting signs: the stores are stocked with objects intended for use at Halloween, many imported from the United States. In shop windows, hollowed-out pumpkins, most made of plastic, with cutout holes that figure eyes, nose, and mouth, beam their ghostly smiles, abetted by the flickering light within. Groups of children come out of schools or private homes disguised as monsters, werewolves, vampires, and extraterrestrial beings. Have we come this far to see an imitation, in third-world gear, of the North American Halloween? Partial reassurance comes from a television program that I watch the same evening in my hotel room. The broadcast features celebrations in private homes in an old district of the city and shows that the traditional custom of raising altars to the souls of the departed is still maintained. The construction of such altars, or *ofrendas*, is elaborate and time consuming, a circumstance that perhaps favors the ascendancy of the customs imported from the North. All the ingeniousness of native craft, with its regional variations, contributes to the making of the altars, which bear sugar skulls painted with gaudy floral motifs among piles of candies, foodstuffs, and images of saints.

A bedazzling altar shown in the television program is the handiwork of an artist, Rafael Alvarez. In his *ofrenda*, native craft and an innovative sense of beauty combine to yield a stunning production that would deserve the praise of sophisticated art critics if it stood side by side with the work of those contemporary artists who blend photography, painting, statuary, and boxes of light. The television reporter is of the same opinion. She asks him: "If your *ofrenda* were kept in a museum for many years, would it increase its effectiveness in attracting the souls of the dead? And what would you say to the souls if you could talk to them?" Alvarez pauses for a minute and replies: "A few years from now I may have to greet them with the words *'Good morning'* uttered in perfect English accent."

This prognosis seems unwarranted the

next day. The *calavera* still reigns supreme. *"Calavera"* is a familiar word that designates the skull, and by extension the whole skeleton. In slang it is known as *calaca*. Skeletons are seen everywhere, but they are regarded with a note of mockery, and therefore are not usually referred to as skeletons, but as *calaveras* or *calacas*. A still greater trivialization may be obtained by the use of the diminutive, which is conveniently produced with the affix *ito* or *ita*. It is a strange Mexican proclivity to tack the diminutive affix, ordinarily reserved for what is pitiable, lovable, or cute, to the frightening and the truculent. Recall the fierce revolutionist Pancho Villa addressing his sinister-looking high command in a hortatory speech before a deadly engagement with the words: *"Amiguitos: Aquí vamos a morirnos todos . . ."* (*"Little* friends: We are all going to die here . . .")

The empire of the skull is undisturbed in this land. On the second of November parents still present their children with skulls made of sugar, or of chocolate, with the respective names inscribed across the frontal bone. Similar gifts are still exchanged between friends, neighbors, relatives, and spouses. One may purchase skeletons made from cardboard or wood, which are made to dance by pulling on strings. A few pesos may buy a whole funeral procession of skeletons, all with chickpea heads, who carry a coffin on their shoulders. In another version, the coffin's lid opens up by pulling a string, which permits another skeleton to pop his head through the casket, like a jack-in-the-box. *Calavera* competitions are held in villages with the intent of holding up the follies of the world to ridicule. The mock skeletons are labeled with inscriptions that give away their identity, otherwise marred by fleshlessness. In 1969, during a competition of this type, a skeleton flaunted a sign that read: "See you later, Onassis. Take care of my widow." But despite their shocking irreverence, these frolics are not the issue of particular, invidious scorn. Starting with local personages, the entire world is the target of satire. The celebration is national, and its unambiguous aim is to ridicule everyone, rich or poor, humble or exalted, foolish or wise.

Appropriately, the film crew heads for a

cemetery. We arrive in the late morning at the town of Xochilmilco, well known for its November celebrations. It is not an easy task to reach the cemetery. On the outside, small stands crowd the street that leads to the main gate. Apparently, Xochilmilcans conceive the River Styx in the shape of an improvised food market. Many of the stands consist of nothing more than wooden benches overhung by a coarse tarpaulin on sticks, and the cook prepares his wares by the sidewalk. Multitudes will spend a great part of the day here; and surely the vendors have wagered that at least some improvident souls will have forgotten to bring refreshments along. Mexican food markets such as this one defy description. Suffice it to say that visitors experience a concerted assault to their senses. The air is pervaded by the smell of glistening tripe and various animal entrails roasting on grills. Mounds of skinned goats' heads rise upon tables. Add to this the commingled street noises and throaty cries of the vendors. The word *visceral* obtrudes spontaneously in the mind, quickened by the strong sensory stimulation; for this word seems to sketch dark

correspondences between the objective reality laid out before us and the inner reaction
it elicits. We sense something obscure, glu-
tinous, smelly, and profoundly integrated to
the spontaneous motions of our internal
organs.

We join the moving frieze of visitors who
wind their way between the stands. Eager
merchants thrust forward the inevitable tor-
tillas on their extended palms, already gar-
nished with meat shreds, and place them
before our eyes while exhorting us to sample
the taco about to be rolled. Their loud sales
pitches join the choral dissonance of the multitude eddying about, now stopping, now
creeping forward.

Inside the cemetery, the spectacle is
stunning. Every tomb, without exception, has
been bedecked with flowers. As far as the eye
can see, there extends an interminable series
of floral displays. In a modern cemetery,
where the tombs lie in symmetrical, orderly
rows, the effect would be striking but somehow wanting in the quaint charm and freshness of the sight now deployed before us.
Here, the place of burial has been created on

hilly terrain with little or no regard for geometry. New graves seem to be assigned whimsically, often lying athwart each other. A straight path is difficult to find, and we advance on a sinuous course to avoid treading upon tombstones. Yet, I suspect some relationship must exist between the amount of burial space, its location, and the purchasing power of the bereaved. For there are humble, small tombs covered with earth, alongside impressive mausoleums complete with granite housing, stone sculptures of crying angels, onyx floral vases, devotional effigies, and so on. Today, however, class distinctions seem blurred by the all-pervading gaiety of the flowers. White, red, yellow, and purple are dominant: chrysanthemums, roses, carnations, daisies, and the traditional *cempazúchil*. To complete the ambience of festivity, children run about playing boisterously, and vendors walk between tombs calling attention to their merchandise with tart cries or shrill whistles. They sell beverages, candies, balloons, whirligigs, and the traditional edible *calaveras* in sugar, chocolate, or amaranth seed.

The filmmakers have a field day. There is so much to record here that after a brief interlude in which I am filmed against this background, I am given leave to withdraw from the scene. The crew turns to the innumerable photogenic aspects of the place, and I to my own private thoughts.

The least that can be said about this place is that it conflicts oddly with the traditional Western idea of a cemetery. The atmosphere is definitely kermis-like. Death is routed, however temporarily. If your idea of a cemetery calls for willow trees with droopy branches against an overcast sky on a gloomy drizzle, this scenery might offend you. If you require a decor fit for the pen of a Romantic poet in a moment of splenetic abstraction, this place is definitely not for you. Here, life flows joyous, uninhibited, and noisy. Dressed in their Sunday frippery, neighbors greet each other, families gossip, parents reprimand unruly children, and all heartily consume the abundant food that on this occasion is anomalously available on hallowed ground. Rarely have I seen the Spanish proverb enacted so forcefully as today: *El muerto al hoyo y el vivo al bollo*—"The dead to the hole, the living to the (sugar) roll."

Shocking? To the foreigner, sometimes. But Mexicans have been inured to these spectacles by an ancient tradition of joking familiarity with death. Whether the roots of this tradition extend into Mexico's pre-Columbian past is a ponderous question much debated in intellectual circles. A satisfactory answer is not available, and the amateur who dabbles in Mexico's ancient cultures risks getting lost in a labyrinthine pantheon of deities with overlapping roles, enigmatic symbolisms, and unpronounceable names.[1] Nevertheless, scholars have clarified certain facts, whose very exoticism spurs the layman's wonder. We may thus be forgiven a quick overview of those Aztec deities that loom largest in the ancient Mexican pantheon and of whom there is cause to suspect some form of continued preternatural influence from the rubble of their ruined temples upon their native soil.

The ideas of earth and death are intimately intertwined in the religion of the ancient Aztecs. This is not surprising, since the earth envelops the dead, receives them in her lap just as a mother might hold her children in a fond embrace. But it is good to remember that our current concept of benevolent maternal love was entirely alien to the earth's attributions in ancient Aztec belief. Actually, the earth was represented as a monster, half fish and half lizard, or as a fantastic frog armed with fangs and claws. Three goddesses are deemed emblematic of the creative and destructive functions of the earth. The distinguished archaeologist Alfonso Caso felt the three were but different aspects of the same deity.[2] Their names are Coatlicue, meaning "she of the skirt of serpents," Cihuacóatl, or "woman of the viper," and Tlazoltéotl, or "goddess of filth."

Tlazoltéotl, also known as Ixcuina, "goddess of filthy things," is represented wearing the skin of a victim, a bandage of unspun cotton suspended with spindles on her headdress, and a black stain on her nose, as if of soot. She eats filth, and therefore has no compunction about ingesting the sins of men, who thereby become cleansed. The rite of confession was practiced with her priests, a fact that must have greatly surprised the early European missionaries. Cihuacóatl is the patroness of women who die in childbirth and also of warriors slain in battle. This is not fortuitous: the Aztecs believed that the newly born became "prisoners of life," and thus a parturient woman was a warrior who took a prisoner. But the best known of the dark goddesses is Coatlicue, probably on account of the dramatic monolith that represents her likeness, which is exhibited today in the National Museum of Anthropology in Mexico City to the great awe of tourists and natives alike. We will have more to say about this imposing lady.

In 1520, Albrecht Dürer saw a collection of "strange and marvelous objects" sent to Charles V from Mexico by Cortes and exhibited in Brussels. Dürer's reaction was one of unalloyed admiration for all those "arms used over there, harnesses, blow-guns, amazing weapons, strange dresses, bed coverlets and all kinds of things made for the use of the people. . . . Nothing have I seen in the course of my life that would have given me such happiness. These were objects of wonderful artistry, and I have much admired the subtle wit of the men of those strange lands."[3] Since this early testimony of a great European artist, the world's reaction to the creations of Aztec symbolic art has been one of perplexed ambivalence. On the one hand, a great number of productions are universally admired for their aesthetic value. On the other hand, many other pieces, although issued from the same culture and clearly representing major productions of its artistic treasury, have been met with indifference, and sometimes with unmitigated horror. The statue of Coatlicue is an example of the latter. Taken in the context of the culture that originated it, there can be no question that this powerful and colossal stone is imbued with an almost inexhaustible symbolic meaning; judged from the vantage point of traditional Western aesthetic canons, it has been variously dubbed a scandal, a nonsensical monstrosity, or a haunting nightmare.

Coatlicue is the mother of the gods, that is to say, of the sun, the moon, and the stars. Her son Huitzilopochtli is the solar deity, who issues every morning from the belly of the old earth goddess. According to the Aztec myth, Coatlicue had already engendered the moon and the stars and lived as a priestess in total chastity. However, while doing her daily domestic chores she found a ball of down, which she swallowed. This ingestion, according to the myth, caused her to become miraculously pregnant. The moon and the stars were so irate over this development, or perhaps so cynically distrustful of the alleged cause of the pregnancy, that they were ready to put their own mother to death. They were about to perform the atrocious crime when Huitzilopochtli was born. Wielding a "fiery serpent" or solar ray he decapitated his sister, the moon, and put the stars to flight. Since that tragic date the heavenly combat must repeat itself daily, and every time the sun god achieves the same victory. However, this triumph does not come easily. The sun god must overcome the numberless stars that dot the firmament. With all his supernatural powers he would be no match for the legions of stars, were it not that the Aztecs, the People of the Sun, nourish their protector god each time, thereby ensuring his reemergence and the gift of a new day for all mankind. It is an unhappy circumstance that the coarse foodstuffs of human beings are inappropriate for the exalted god. His nutrition depends entirely on a constant supply of a precious liquid, the sap of life, "jade water," or as we say today, human blood.

The need for human sacrifice took on an urgent cast. The consequences of its omission would be simply catastrophic, horrendous, and unthinkable: nothing less than breaking the continuity of life on earth. The sacrificial ritual has been described many times in all its ghastly details.[4] Briefly, the victim was placed with his back on a round, large sacrificial stone or *techcatl*, his limbs securely held by priests, while the officiating priest slashed his upper abdomen, just below the ribs, deftly using a flint knife, the *tecpatl*. The priest then plunged his hand into the open wound, and maneuvering his knife tore the heart from its attachments—"broke the heart strings," in the expression of the chronicler Sahagún, who remarked incongruously that the avulsed organ was offered to the sun god "for the space of an Ave Maria," after placing it inside an urn. The lifeless cadaver was thrown down the steps of the pyramid on which the sacrifice was conducted to clear the way for another sacrifice; hundreds and, in the exaggerated claims of some conquistadors, thousands, could be conducted in one day.

Scholars have observed that the choice of sacrificial technique was not fortuitous. Men have made shameful proof of brutality in all countries and at all times; certainly ways of torturing and killing have been fertile grounds for sadistic ingeniousness. In this context, Aztec sacrifices do not appear to have been devised as torture, but as a means to produce copious hemorrhages. Surgeons today greatly fear the slightest accidental nick in the inferior vena cava. To suddenly rip this vein, and to tear at the same time the great vessels emerging from the heart, the aorta and the pulmonary artery and veins, would produce huge spurts of blood in seconds. This horrible fact inclines scholars to believe that the ritual was deliberately chosen by the Aztecs to secure the most dramatic and abundant of hemorrhages, in keeping with the need to spill the precious liquid that alone could ensure the fertility of the earth and abet the progress of the sun god's course. As his passage through the skies ended, he was believed to undertake a journey in the shadowy underworld, from which he would emerge daily—if properly assisted by his votaries—to inundate the world with light.

The statue that represents the sun god's mother, Coatlicue, is a creation of great expressive force. She wears a skirt of intertwined serpents, which is held in place by another snake in the guise of a belt. She sports a collar of amputated hands and hearts, ending up in a human skull at waist level, although it cannot be truthfully said that a waist is discernible in this massive, squarish stone block. Instead of hands and feet she has huge vulturelike claws, reminding us that, like a vulture, she is the insatiable "eater of filth" who feeds on corpses, thus fulfilling her role as earth goddess. Her breasts are pendulous, because she has breast-fed generations of men, also in her role as earth goddess. In vain do we look for her face. Her head is actually made of two serpent heads facing each other, which presumably symbolize paired jets of blood after decapitation. The two serpent heads form a hallucinatory, symmetrical visage resulting from the close contact of two ophidian profiles. Strips of red leather hung with shells, the attribute of earth divinities, are represented streaming from her back.

Imagine the men of the Enlightenment, accustomed to the delicate preciosity of Watteau and Fragonard, or to the airy wit of Voltaire, coming across the massive, barbaric bulk of lady Coatlicue. This is precisely what happened on the morning of August 13, 1790, when city workers digging in the central square of Mexico City struck their shovels against the petrous body of the dark goddess. They disinterred her and, not without apprehension, wiped off the muddy clay that stuck to her surface with the tenacity of a three-centuries-old embrace.

Shocked as they were, her discoverers were nonetheless men of the Enlightenment, suffused with respect for the "monuments of antiquity." Most of them had read the works of the French encyclopedists, albeit in ex-

purgated editions shorn of dangerous passages that might inflame seditious sentiment
injurious to the Spanish crown. Many, it is
now clear, unafraid to jeopardize bodily in-
tegrity for the love of learning, had managed
to read original versions smuggled into the
country. Among the group of learned professors who canvassed the huge monolith
with their magnifying glasses, inch by inch,
was a grave gentleman named Antonio de
León y Gama. He managed to write an erudite monograph on the extraordinary finding.
Those were happy times when to "publish or
perish" had not yet become an obsessive
preoccupation for academics: his monograph
was published in Rome some fourteen years
after it had been written.

The ruling Spanish viceroy, Conde de
Revilla Gigedo, also prided himself on being
a man of the Enlightenment. Attuned to the
spirit of the times, he decreed that Coatlicue
should repose in a stately hall of Mexico's
Royal and Pontifical University, amidst plas-
ter casts and statues donated by the Spanish
crown. Presumably, "she of the skirt of serpents" would contribute to promote the aes-

thetic education of art students. But we may
well imagine how she must have looked surrounded by reproductions of the Lacoon,
Psyche, assorted nymphs, and other classic
Greco-Roman models. I suppose it was like
placing in the middle of a courtesan's bou-
doir in Louis XV style some anguished, neurotic contemporary painting: say, Edvard
Munch's *The Scream*. Little wonder that, before a year had passed, a group of university
professors recommended that the Aztec goddess should be reburied where she had been
found. Academics were then commonly ec-
clesiastics; among the reasons put forth in
favor of the decision was the warning, not
altogether unfounded, that the continued
presence of the goddess aboveground could
revive pagan sentiments in an Indian population still imperfectly assimilated to the high
ideals of the Christian dogmas.

And so, the earth goddess was buried
again. Earth to earth. She remained under-
ground until the following century when the
German savant Alexander von Humboldt,
who possibily had read the descriptive monograph, visited Mexico. The illustrious visitor

asked to see the statue. The authorities complied, but once the scientist had assuaged his intellectual curiosity, the idol was once more lowered to its dismal pit. There Coatlicue remained until Mexico became an independent nation eager to trace her roots. The statue was unearthed once again and kept in various temporary domiciles within government buildings. Still, it was difficult for all to come to terms with this unsettling presence. The goddess continued to excite astonishment, puzzlement, revulsion, fright, and scientific curiosity. At last she came to occupy the place she still has, a place of honor in the major Aztec hall of Mexico's National Museum of Anthropology.

Gradually, Coatlicue was despoiled of her most terrifying powers. Long gone are Aztec worshipers who daubed her face with blood and surrounded her hideous body with volutes of incense smoke. Fanatic Spanish friars who approached her holding a crucifix at the end of their extended arms, while singing the versets of the Gospel, are no longer to be seen. Her votaries are now anthropologists, archaeologists, art critics, and philosophers. Artists, especially, are among the faithful. For they perceive a fantastic being emerging from a remote past, and yet strangely accoutred with features that appeal to the modern mind. Octavio Paz has remarked that in Coatlicue's statue there is a disdain for anthropomorphism, a complete disregard for the rules of classic aestheticism that have dominated Western art, and a juxtaposition of highly realistic components— eyes, hands, writhing serpents—in a whole that is not a reality, but an abstraction.[5] In sum, artists see in Coatlicue a powerful example of modernist abstractionism.

Scholarly monographs will continue to be written. The formidable monolith is shown by modern interpreters to be a "hive of symbols," in the expression of Justino Fernandez, one of the most erudite and sensitive of the modern votaries of the dark goddess.[6] To detect such symbols may require, however, that we cast away all the preconceptions and mental conditioning imposed on us by the contemporary world. Thus, each new era will see something new, provided a fresh glance is directed at the awesome sculpture. Whether this sculpture should be ranked with works of art is itself an unanswered question. For what was art to the society that created it? Aesthetic emotion, as we now understand it, probably was never regarded as an isolated value in pre-Columbian Mexico. Art was then but one facet of the innumerable magico-religious manifestations that informed every strand of daily life; a means to commune with otherworldly forces; a handle on the sacred. There could be no *objet d'art* such as we expect to see in collections and museums to-day. Every artistic production was simulta-neously and unavoidably a ritual object, an adjunct to religious worship. Octavio Paz, again, has put it most eloquently: "Coatlicue is simultaneously a charade, a syllogism, and a presence that condenses a *mysterium tre-mendum. . . .* A cube of stone that is at the same time a metaphysics."[7]

If, in fact, Coatlicue is a treatise on meta-physics, it seems to me a rather depressing one. There is a shudder in this philosophy. Reality is at one time maker and destroyer, impassive generator and merciless crusher: "like a great mouth," writes Paz, "hungry and empty, that will end up by devouring us all, tomb and womb at the same time." Its cosmology specified a unique place for human blood, conveyor of the only energy capable of keeping the constellations moving, the sun rising, and the seeds germinating. Its vision of the world and of life outlined a precarious equilibrium, always on the verge of hecatomb and major disaster. Mankind could be ransomed through ritual wars, and universal disaster could be averted through human sacrifices. As to aesthetics, it is easy to see that such a philosophical system had to produce aesthetic forms that incorporated the horrible, the ghastly, or the grotesque. The Aztec vision of the world strikes a raw nerve in the sensitivity of an observer of modern life.

Contemporary mankind lives in the consciousness that nuclear catastrophe may put an end to existence on this planet. The ancient Aztecs, for different reasons, sensed the imminence of destruction. Jacques Soustelle suggests that the high development of astronomy in the ancient Mesoamerican civilizations may have been prompted by a desire to predict, from observation of the stars, the occurrence of disasters to come. In framing the feeling proper to this philosophical system, the ancient bards soared to a universal plane; in their utterances we recognize ourselves regardless of our nationality or social condition. In an Aztec poem translated by León-Portilla,[8] we read:

> *The Giver of life mocks us.*
> *O, our friends,*
> *Our hearts are trusting,*
> *But he mocks us.*

A depressing musing that stemmed from a pessimistic philosophy, this is strangely reminiscent of Gloucester's oft-quoted lamentation in Shakespeare's *King Lear:*

As flies to wanton boys, are we to the gods,
They kill us for their sport. (IV, i, 38)

The Aztec poet-philosopher Netzaualcoyotl uttered sighs of lamentation for the delusive worth of earthly life that might stand on equal footing with the highest lyrical expressions of European wistfulness on the brevity of human existence:

Do we really live on earth?
Not forever on earth, only a little here:
Though it be jade, it crumbles;
Though it be gold, it breaks;
Though it be feathers of quetzal, it tears.
Not forever on earth, only a little here.

Whether the ancient ideas are relevant to contemporary Mexican life is an idle question. A good part of Mexico's intelligentsia has pondered this problem for generations, without reaching consensus. The Aztec language and religion, those two central pillars of the collective identity, were utterly destroyed. Christian churches uprear their towers and spires where pagan temples once stood. It is no easy task to determine whether under the foundation, fathoms below, the old ideas still rally, like a routed army.

On the surface, the two features that strike the observer as unique to the Mexican way of death are merrymaking and fatalistic impassiveness. Are these the two ancestral attitudes that unexpectedly resurge from the unconscious, like wrecks in the tide? Let the experts decide. The nonprofessional can only form subjective impressions. Mine, on this sunny morning spent in a cemetery disguised as a fair, compel me to agree with those who repeat that Mexicans obstinately refuse to take death seriously, at least on the first week of November. The European *danse macabre*, elsewhere conducted as a stately pavane intended to edify, becomes here a frenzied *zapateado*, with all in attendance clapping, hooting, and joining the dance. The skeleton leads the way, and nobody seems to be surprised. It is impossible to overlook the fact that for the ancient Mexicans the skeleton had none of the lugubrious attributes that we have annexed to it: according to Paul Westheim, the skull was a common ornamental motif that was used to embellish simple objects, and thus it is not surprising that archaeologists find skulls engraved on everyday household utensils such as pots and pans.[9]

Today, a frolicsome attitude toward death persists in language. Derisive epithets, perhaps used as a means to disguise an unbearable reality, are utilized in every country. However, I believe Mexico's death-related slang must figure among the most varied, ingenious, and acid. About three decades ago, a scholar collected many of these popular expressions in a book.[10] They are still current, and many are diversified. Thus, all Mexicans understand that sentences that begin with the expression *"Se lo llevó . . . ,"* meaning "He/She was carried away by . . .," signify that the person alluded to passed away. To die, therefore, is to be carried away by a number of agents, which may be as varied as there are possible subjects in the sentence. Agents commonly doing the carrying away include:

The Bald One *(la pelona)*	Judas
Big Head *(la cabezona)*	The trap *(la trampa)*
Smiley *(la sonrisas)*	The horn *(el cuerno)*
Big Teeth *(la dientona)*	The devil *(el diablo)*
Mary Sickles *(María Guadaña)*	Santa Claus

Goat's Feet *(patas de cabra,* that is, the devil)

Rooster's Feet *(patas de gallo,* presumably a thin-footed agent, like a skeleton)

Death as renunciation and surrender, as in "giving up one's life," or "giving up the ghost," is expressed in irreverent phrases that include:

> To return the equipment
> To turn in one's tennis shoes
> To turn in one's driver's license

Death as departure, as in the English "to come out feet first," becomes:

> To move to Calaca City
> To reach the nineteenth hole
> To move to the Valley of the Bald
> To elope with the Skinny One
> To have a rendezvous with Smiley,
> Big Teeth, etc.

Merriment alone does not characterize the Mexican attitude. There is also an element of fatalism. The Aztecs lived with the pervasive feeling of the futility of human aspirations; their pessimistic philosophy must have endowed them with plenty of resigned acceptance of man's vulnerability. Moreover, it is hardly necessary to invoke the intervention of highly debatable pre-Columbian atavisms. Stoicism and resignation are bulwarks against misfortune, and Mexico has known repeated large-scale catastrophe. Last in the dismal series was an earthquake that toppled an estimated three thousand buildings in minutes; man-made woe, usually less paroxysmal, has been no less fierce. The fourth horseman of the Apocalypse has charged again and again; and it is hardly surprising that the survivors should have evolved defense mechanisms against indiscriminate annihilation. As in other latitudes, dark humor and a shrug of the shoulders have expressed this powerless resignation. In Mexico, the expression *"Ya le tocaba,"* the equivalent of "his number was up" or "his turn finally arrived," often condenses the only possible reaction in the face of ineluctable doom.

In the Western conception, human life is a precious gift to be defended at all costs. The Aztecs viewed life as a prison, whose chief merit was its transitoriness. Each time human life seems wasted, Western civilization reacts with boundless indignation and angry outcry. The moral sense is in a dudgeon: the outrageous violation should not have happened, cannot be tolerated, must never happen again. Mexican fatalism replies with *"Ya le tocaba,"* his turn was foreordained, and it has come to pass.

José Vasconcelos, an illustrious Mexican intellectual, narrated an episode illustrative of the preposterous extremes attained by this notion.[11] During Mexico's revolutionary struggle, Urbina, a lieutenant in Pancho Villa's forces, invited his *compadre* to dinner. There was abundant libation. Toward the end of the meal, the spirituous fumes had intensified the feeling of friendship, as they are wont to do in the early stages of intoxication. His left arm draped over the shoulders of his *compadre*, Urbina continued to toast with his right hand, alternatively to the greater glory of the revolution, and to the undying friendship of comrades-at-arms. The room was very hot. Urbina's *compadre* felt like wiping off his face, and to this effect made a movement to draw his *mascada*, a red scarf styled by ranchers in that area, from his pocket. Alas, Urbina interpreted this motion as an attempt to draw a gun. Without a moment's hesitation he drew first and shot the man through the heart. As the victim's body was being laid out on a mat, it became apparent that he clutched a red scarf in his hand. Urbina, still drunk, broke out in sobs, and with sincere grief exclaimed: "My poor *compadrito!* You see, *ya le tocaba.*"

Of Skulls in a Heap and Soft Parts in Glass Jars

All physicians encounter in their practice the phenomenon of termination of life. It is a moment of great disheartenment when all hopes of routing the progress of disease are dashed. The ardor of life-sustaining efforts is suddenly extinguished. The intensity of the struggle, at its highest pitch moments before, instantly winds down. For most physicians this is the time when "no more can be done"; a humbling experience from which they walk away contrite, unnerved, and profoundly frustrated. But there is one physician for

whom this phenomenon carries a wider significance, reaching beyond frustration and
despondency and, in a way, transcending
them. This is the pathologist, whose task, in
effect, has just begun. The slow and deep
sonance of death's knell, which in others
raises alarm, fear, or grief, summons the pathologist to begin his task. And the corpse,
image of terror for most men, symbol of the
supreme defeat for healers, remains for the
pathologist the cipher of the living state: a
cabalistic text spelling, in key, the mysteries
of life and health.

It seems natural that in a country that
portrays the dead with gusto and that sed-
ulously exalts the souls of the departed, the
pathologist should figure prominently in the
ceremonious and convivial festivities. So it is
in Mexico. Here the Day of the Dead is a
national festivity, and my colleagues, only
half in jest, have made it also "the day of
the pathologist." This circumstance greatly
amuses our film director, who wishes to see,
and to film, the celebration. In vain I represent to him that all I recollect from my
student days is an abbreviation of the work-

ing schedule on that day, or a quiet gathering
of muted conviviality. He still insists on the
filmic potential of the event.

We are fortunate to secure the cooperation of an eminent Mexican pathologist, Dr.
A. Rodriguez, chief of the department of pathology of the General Hospital of Mexico
City. To please the film director, he has prepared a showy ceremony. The department is
housed in a spacious two-story building
within the hospital's extensive grounds. On
the lower floor, an ample hall houses large
showcases reaching almost to the ceiling,
cases that contain a collection of anatomical
specimens in glass jars, carefully arrayed for
the teaching of medical students and trainees.
The choice of site was determined after no
little haggling, but it will enhance the film's
visual quality: colored paper cutouts have
been hung between glass cabinets, and an
altar or *ofrenda* has been raised in a corner.
According to tradition, the altar is a table
covered by a cloth and bearing fruits, dain-
ties, beverages, and votive lamps. The popular belief maintains that the souls of the
dead are licensed once a year to descend upon

the earth and enjoy the celebration in the company of friends and relatives.

The Mexican tradition of *ofrendas*, like so many others in this hallucinatory land, is a mestizo custom: the syncretic fusion of Catholic rites imposed by Spain and elements of the indigenous religious practices preexisting the arrival of Catholicism. Observance of these customs reaffirms what we all know: in Mexico the dead are not quite gone, and death remains a living personage, the bearer and harbinger of itself. It used to be possible to observe the pertinent ceremonies in their pristine splendor in small villages near Mexico City. In the small town of Mizquic, a former islet in the now desiccated Lake Chalco, the celebration of the Day of the Dead is still enacted with enthusiasm—and with an eye, I am afraid, for the ever-growing number of tourists.[1] The unbroken link between the living and the dead was vividly demonstrated by the reminiscences of an old woman of this town. She recalled how, in the old days, her mother would set up the altar, diligently tidy up the house, and make sure that the table was set before the church bells started sound-

ing. Then, on the afternoon of the second of
November, she would go out to the street and
actually talk to the invisible souls in these
terms:

"Come in, blessed souls of my father,
my mother, and my sisters. Please, come in.
How did you do this year? Are you pleased
with your living relatives? In the kitchen we
have tamales, tostadas, pumpkin with honey,
apples, oranges, sugarcane, chicken broth, a
great deal of salt, and even a little tequila,
so you may drink. Are you happy with what
we have? My sons worked very hard this year
so we could offer you this feast, as usual. Tell
me, how is Saint Joseph? Did he receive the
Masses we ordered for him?"

The old woman could talk to the
"blessed souls" for hours. It is not difficult
to see how her daughter, impressed by the
vividness of this intercourse, would endeavor
to preserve the tradition. She must have felt
that her mother's soul would never rest in
peace, unless her post-death solace were secured by continuing a periodic dialogue she
took so much in earnest.

I begin to grow worried as our ceremony's preparation advances. I almost regret having spoken to the film director about the day of the pathologist. In place of a quiet celebration, or perhaps no celebration at all, we now have a rich *ofrenda*, lavish decorations, and special scenic effects. The power of the cameras! The ideal of documentary filmmaking is to surprise human behavior at its source and to capture it as it bubbles up from its fount. But short of employing deception and the techniques of international spies, this goal must remain a sort of torture of Tantalus. For no sooner is the camera bracketed upon a subject than he becomes an actor on the stage, posing, declaiming, and mindful of presenting only his "best angle." In film, as in physics, Heisenberg's principle of uncertainty applies: an ideal observation of a natural phenomenon is impossible, because the universe is so constructed that our recording instruments must introduce changes, thereby modifying the selfsame phenomenon we wished to apprehend.

Another worry, and not the least one, is the choice of site. A segment of the public, disposed to maintain stiff norms of taste in all that pertains to death, is apt to think ill of a group of medical specialists "introducing levity into the morgue," as someone remarked. However, this fear is unfounded. Levity is not the right word; and the morgue is not entered at any time. The intent is to honor the souls of the departed in the style of the country where they had their last abode. *They*, assuredly, would not be offended. I rather think the souls of the departed do not judge us according to our own criteria. Incorporeal spirits, once disburdened from the miseries of the world, probably do not form opinions of us based on our intellectual merit, or even our moral values. If they did, they could not bear us, and the ceremony would be pointless. I wager that from their heavenly vantage point they see us as we are, and as they formerly were: weak bundles of anguish and suffering, held together by constitutional heedlessness. I hope they do so, at least, for only thus could they have any sympathy for us.

And what better than that such a ceremony should take place in a hospital and be organized by pathologists? The blessed souls,

again, would not mind. We were the last to
minister to their earthly needs; the last to
take charge of each body after it was dis-
engaged from the soul. As pathologists, our
efforts lacked the drama of those of other
physicians. But we tried to help. In many
cases it was thanks to us that a diagnosis was
established. Such is our charge: to unveil
the order hidden behind apparent chaos. As
to the site chosen for this festivity, nothing
seems more justified. It is in places such as
hospitals, prisons, and concentration camps
that the spectacle of human suffering would
remind the deceased of the pain of the living,
and confirm them in the conviction that it is
infinitely better to have left to join the eternal
cycle of nature's transmutations.

These considerations do not clear all my
worries. I do not know what will be expected
of me during the ceremony. I certainly do not
feel able to emulate the verve of the old
woman in Mizquic if asked to address the
souls of the departed. I could, at best, put to
them some questions. Something like this:

"Blessed souls, please come in. Make
yourselves at home in this precinct. From
your heavenly station you can see all, and

you probably know that a hospital is not the worst repository of human despair. The shantytowns of our cities, the dungeons, the prisons, the chambers of torture, the battle-fields: all the sites where human misery and shame seek to elude the light of day are open to your vision. Tell us, dear blessed souls, if it is not true that the enormous investment of natural energy that must constantly be applied to sustain life seems a bit absurd to you, and if it is not true that it is a relief to see it finally abated in your individual beings.

"As to ourselves, we were convinced that from the study of your mortal remains we could derive a lesson useful to others. Tell us if there is any merit in our viewpoint. Is it true that each individual lives only a dream, at a vertiginous speed, and is then instan-taneously effaced to leave the place to oth-ers—others for whose good we must keep striving? We wish to know if this assumption is correct, that the individual counts for noth-ing, or next to nothing, and that the only things worth preserving are the general fea-tures of mankind—the broad brushstrokes—which are to subsist in the species.

"But if you cannot answer these queries,

come in, anyway, and share with us this banquet, which the Mexican tradition allows you once every November. Excuse our coarse method of enjoying these tamales and these tostadas: you remember that we must gulp them down. Disembodied spirits that you are, you must be satisfied with only the perceptions of smell, the most subtile of the senses."

Fortunately, there is no need for me to make such a speech. A program has been improvised. Dr. Rodriguez, our host, addresses his staff gathered around the altar. After some generalities and commonplaces on the nature of the occasion, he announces that I was a special guest and proceeds to unveil my *calavera*. This word has different meanings. Its primary acceptations are the skull and the skeleton. By a strange association of ideas, whose nature escapes me, it has come to designate a philanderer or playboy. In still another meaning, unique to Mexico and now intended, it refers to an epitaph or obituary written in verse. *Calaveras* of this type are a well-known tradition. They are printed in newspapers or sold in loose-leaf binding and serve to lampoon the notables of the land. Politicians, actors, singers, athletes, or anyone who has attained some public notoriety may open the newspaper one morning to find his or her own funeral notice couched in rhyming stanzas of variable poetic merit. Always, however, in a biting satirical tone.

I acknowledge my own *calavera* in the same spirit in which it was offered. (It was, to be truthful, of indifferent poetic merit.) Next, the attendees identify similar notices tacked on a bulletin board. Virtually every member of the staff has the ambiguous pleasure of reading his or her own versified obituary. An anonymous hand with an undeniable gift for cartoon drawing has graced each production with the skeletized caricature of its subject. It is a cause for clamorous mirth to identify one's own. The cameras do not rest while surprising the revelers in this activity.

The tradition of *calaveras* functions as an outlet for popular discontent. The targets are individual personalities, corruption, politics, and virtually anything that strikes the author's fancy. The theme may be impersonal and abstract. I quote from memory an old *calavera* that was circulated many years ago:

> *Calavera es el inglés,*
> *Calavera el mexicano,*
> *El emperador Maximiliano*
> *Y el Pontífice Romano.*
>
> *El líder máximo de la nación,*
> *Duques, reyes, consejales,*
> *En la tumba son iguales:*
> *Calaveras del montón.*

I can only imperfectly translate: "Skull is the Englishman / And skull is the Mexican / Emperor Maximilian / And the Pontiff Roman. / The country's powers-that-be / Duke, king, sheriff / In the grave equally shall be / Skulls in a heap."

Here we recognize the ancient preoccupation with death as leveler, a theme by no means exclusive to a given time or country. Already in Lucian's *Dialogues of the Dead* one hears the skulls of the deceased holding a conversation whose consequence is

the demolition of the vanity of earthly glory.
The handsome and the ugly, the clever and
the dull are now "skulls in a heap." No one
can boast any longer of excelling the others
in any quality, "unless it be in brittleness."
All flash the same toothy smile, exhibit the
same vacant orbits, parade around the same
snub nose . . .

Other lands, other epochs, produced
striking shows centered upon the idea of
death. The Italian Renaissance originated
magnificent spectacles and did not shun the
macabre. In a carnival organized by Piero di
Cosimo in 1551, a huge black cart, drawn
by black bisons and crowded with human
bones and white crosses, carried an enormous
Death wielding a sickle and surrounded by
tombs.[2] At each station where the cart
stopped, the tomb slabs parted, and the public could see frightening beings simulating
decomposing cadaver, emerging from the
graves. There followed other terrible personages, or "death masks," who carried torches
and sang hymns to intensify the horror of the
spectators. This was a grandiose theatrical
exultation, a sophisticated *mise en scène* wor-

thy of the Italian Renaissance, carefully calculated to excite collective shudders in
crowds sensitized to the idea of death. In
Rome, I recognized a hint of the feelings
stirred by this pageantry, a mixture of fas-
cination and revulsion, upon discovering in
the magnificent temple of Santa Maria Mag-
giore the richly ornamented mortal despoils
of a high prelate of the Church exhibited in
a glazed coffin: a silver mask hides the discarnate skull; a bejeweled miter tops the bald
crown; and sumptuous weeds, embroidered
with gold thread and dotted with gems, ad-
here snugly to the skeletized remains.

Thus, the ideas embodied in Mexican
folklore cannot be said to be original. What
strikes us as unique is the tone, the sincere
ring of festive humor and fun. The rich European imagery of death—Dürer's engrav-
ings, Holbein's woodcuts of the *danse
macabre*—is clearly meant to affright us and
at the same time to compel us to repent of
our sins. The symbolic representation of
death, the skeleton, seems to say: "Remember that soon you shall be like I am. Meditate
on the vanity of your life in the world. Your

destruction, your putrefaction, is very close to you. It is right here, it touches you!'" The Mexican skeleton, in striking contrast, is no spook. It is a policeman, a city dandy, a hired ranch hand, or a bartender. "It is neither more horrible nor more frightening than men," wrote Paul Westheim. A *calavera*, though a skeleton, poses no threats.

It may be argued that all this is affectation and pose; that Mexicans disguise the universal fear of death under the trappings of hilarity. So be it; it is still necessary to acknowledge that the disguise works wonderfully well. The skeletons that populate Mexico in early November do not address us with pathetic appeals. They never adopt dramatic poses; nor can we hear them intoning mournful dirges. We hear from them no solemn injunctions to repent, no preaching, no somber reminders of our need for moral regeneration. Caustic wit, biting irony, and sarcasm are their only weapons. They nettle us, and the rest they leave to our discretion.

Perhaps all this is just as well. For if the souls of the departed were not the jolly, carefree bunch that they are deemed to be in this land, but the ghastly, vindictive phantasms that they are reputed to be elsewhere, our pathologists' celebration would have been impossible. We are surrounded by bodily parts preserved in liquid fixative; each one of these specimens once belonged in a body-soul binomial. Who knows, if the blessed souls took umbrage at our occupation, how dissectors might have fared today. A Christian tradition long regarded bodily parts with contempt: only the soul, which is eternal, was deemed worthy of concern. But this hierarchy was not always present in the minds of Christians. Saint Augustine, like most people, held corpse handlers in contempt. In his *City of God* he had harsh words for anatomists "who ruthlessly applied themselves to carving up dead bodies . . . with little regard for humanity" (Bk. 22, ch. 24). Pope Boniface VIII plainly excommunicated crusaders who transported the skeletons of their fallen comrades for burial in the homeland. I can only hope that the blessed souls that tenanted the anatomic specimens here displayed do not share this animosity toward dissectors.

The film director instructs us to walk

between the glass cabinets, and this scene must be filmed many times on account of unwanted glare that interferes with optimal photography. Dr. Rodriguez and I make the ordered perambulation, repeating casual comments along the way. The orderly parade of rows of preserved brains, stomachs, lungs, and uteruses brings to mind the witty jab of Richard Seltzer, the surgeon-writer, on the compulsion that drives pathologists to store diseased organs removed at surgery or autopsy. He remarked that if a pathologist had witnessed the martyrdom of Saint Sebastian, the liver of the martyr might still exist today on some shelf, immersed in formalin and bearing an identification label saying: Liver of saint, with characteristic lacerations produced by arrows.

This compulsion is, indeed, of more than passing interest, since one does not become a collector of bodily parts in the same way as one turns philatelist or coin collector. A curator's task is never easy: he must come to terms with prohibitions of religious dogmas, prejudices, his own inner fears, and the ceaseless inroads of organic decomposition. Nevertheless, and in spite of secular difficulties, anatomical dissection and preservation of organs have been assiduously performed. The reason usually stated, that anatomical specimens contribute to better understanding and teaching of medical concepts, rings true in a unique way for those of us who actually perform the dissections. For a specimen has this singular power: it tenders a strong, vivid representation that the mind seizes immediately. The sight of a scarred organ suggests chronicity; of a perforated viscus, the role of abrupt mechanisms of overwhelming potency. It is inevitable, upon seeing, to immediately conclude. The immediate consequence of looking at a specimen is not a deductive chain. A specimen does not produce a thin line of arguments, bordering on the verge of fallacy, which reasoning must carefully follow risking the headlong tumble at every step. No: the imagination is goaded forward and leaps like a nervous steed. It jumps, so to speak, ahead of reason; and the one must soon catch up and take control of the other if any progress is to be made. Epistemologists have yet to explain the curious phenomenon that seeing makes us guess, and—the record of the pathologic anatomy is there to attest it—often guess aright.

Assume Seltzer's "liver of Saint Sebastian" is preserved in this collection, its resplendent aureole undimmed by centuries-long submersion in 10 percent buffered formalin. Visual inspection of the organ riddled with arrows would suggest a swarm of ideas: the state of warfare technology of the era, the positions of the archers, the sufferings of the martyr. A modern pathologist imbued with the scientific spirit would caution us against the dangers of pure morphology and would amply warn us against jumping to conclusions that cannot be tested directly, as by planned experiments. But no one, not even the most recalcitrant denigrator of pathologic anatomy, would conclude, from observation of the saintly liver, that this organ had the ability to synthesize and secrete arrows.

Still, the practice of amassing anatomical specimens has had variable fortunes. Its halcyon days may be traced to the Enlightenment. Anatomists of the time perfected methods of vascular injection that permitted bodily parts to be preserved and then exhibited as the handiwork of a wise Creator, in accordance with the prevailing philosophical views. The craze for dissection reached its peak then. Anatomical specimens were flaunted, like heirlooms handed down in the family. Frederick Ruysch (1638–1731) bequeathed to posterity a museum that contained not only organs and limbs, but entire bodies of infants and adults preserved by fixatives of his own invention. Skeletons were arranged in dramatic positions; cadavers with muscles well displayed were posed in theatrical gestures; others were provided with pocket handkerchiefs made of pieces of peritoneum and were adorned at the wrist and the neck with fragments of membranous tissue to simulate the lace, frills, and ruffles then fashionable. Peter the Great was so impressed upon first seeing this collection in 1698 that on his second visit to Amsterdam, he bought it whole. The collection, and a description of the methods used to prepare the specimens, was transported to Saint Petersburg. Bernard Siegfried Albinus (1697–

1770), of Leyden, continued the tradition initiated by Ruysch.[3]

The specimens prepared by these anatomists were injected intravascularly with a mixture of red-colored wax, mutton fat, and turpentine. It is a tribute to their technical ingenuity that many such specimens still exist. Their bizarre flair for display has been captured in powerful photographs with unsettling impact, eerily evocative and nightmarish, by the American artist-photographer Rosamond Purcell. One of these specimens consists of a child's upper extremity, carefully clad in a laced sleeve; the hand is made to hold a human eye by the optic nerve in a gesture that brings to mind the dainty posture of a lady holding a flower by the stem.[4]

The bent for the bizarre is gone. No such odd taste is detectable in the specimens that surround us. Ostensibly, they have been prepared strictly for the purpose of collecting scientific information and for teaching students. But all has yet to be said about the determinants of this practice. Knowledge as an instrument to dominate nature is the unquestioned faith of our times. One wonders whether to enclose diseased organs in jars may partake of the symbolism of capturing evil genii in bottles: the evil powers, thus made subservient, may work their potency on our behalf, like the relics of saints. Nor is the parallel between treasuring relics and hoarding medical specimens altogether far-fetched. Like relics, the value of anatomical specimens has been lowered from an unreasonable pinnacle. In medieval times, Church authorities commissioned an agent in Rome to purchase Saint Augustine's arm for the amount of one hundred talents of silver and one of gold. Much later, apparently for different motives, an honored member of the medical profession, John Hunter, paid five hundred pounds to obtain the body of an Irish giant, which he procured by illegal means.[5] Like other anatomists of past times, Hunter stood under suspicion of criminal behavior: they were ready to engage in the most unseemly practices if the reward was a desired specimen. The rarer, the better. One is reminded of the monks of Soissons, who based their pride in the preposterous claim of possessing the navel "and other parts less decent" of the body of Christ!

But times change. With the Reformation, the market for relics shrunk. A tooth of Saint Agatha or the instruments of torture that touched the body of a holy martyr now commanded entirely different sums of money in Lutheran Germany and in Catholic Italy. Disraeli quoted Lord Herbert as saying, in his *Life of Henry VIII*, that after the dissolution of the monasteries in England a piece of Saint Andrew's finger was not accepted as payment by officers of the crown.[6] The king's commissioners returned the holy relic upon the closing of a monastery: they preferred to pay the debts rather than to keep the finger of the glorious saint. Alas, this melancholy disillusion now touches anatomical museums. Contemporary science believes life's flow too wondrous and delicate a process for anything of substance to be learned by preserving lumps of dead matter. For, make no mistake, this is what pathologists do: they arrest the precarious equilibrium, brutally collapsing it with harsh chemical fixatives, and often literally "freezing" it cold.

In less sophisticated times the roughness of the methods mattered little. Clinical medicine was still, as Foucault formulated, "an extension of the gaze." The physician who examined a patient exerted the mind's eye to see disordered organs as cause of the symptoms. He would try to imagine forms and textures; to "see" shaggy pleural surfaces rubbing against each other to produce the harsh sound, as of sliding sheets of leather, perceived on auscultation; to imagine how the blood, squeezing rhythmically across hardened aortic valves, would yield the intermittent vibratory sensation gathered by the fingers applied against the patient's thorax. But the conception of clinical medicine as "extended gaze" is largely superseded. Those of us who were trained four decades ago approached the patient as hunters alert to "see," in the brake and thicket of symptoms, enlarged hearts and knobby livers. Today, medical students are instructed to represent in their inner gaze dancing molecules and disordered sequences of nucleic acid.

I will not be the one to regret this. When Ramón y Cajal opened the eyes of the scientific world to the astounding microscopic

complexity of the nervous system, his igno-
rant detractors, anatomists of the old school,
pointed out with sarcasm that he versed himself in "celestial anatomy." If today gross and
microscopic pathology must make way for
their molecular counterpart, so be it. Let the
few remaining shelves with fixed organs be
destroyed forever. But I am curious and
would like to be able to see, a century or two
from now, how diseased bodily parts unfit to
be used as spares are dealt with by the pathologists of the future. Therefore, I hereby
manifest my wish to be buried, when my time
comes, in such a plot of land as admits ap-
plications for temporary leaves of absence
from residents. Thus would I be able to enjoy
a yearly Mexican fiesta within a pathology
laboratory, satisfying at once lust for life
and scientific curiosity. If it is not too much
trouble, place me inside one of those Greco-
Roman sarcophagi that one sees in museums,
with elaborate carvings on all sides. For in
the interval between fiestas, during my progressive dissolution, I should like to feel
hemmed in by the images of life in the style
of the ancients: youths picking grapes and

sounding lyres in a forest of intertwining vines; gods and goddesses disporting themselves with Olympian abandon; hairy satyrs chasing nymphs, and even in active congress with their coveted prey.

Two Unrecorded Scenes

I have a free day in Mexico City. The film director and his crew will be busy capturing some of the many visually striking scenes that may be encountered here during the first days of November. Left on my own, I roam the streets and recognize some familiar places with that bittersweet mixture of nostalgia, tender enthusiasm, and disappointment that is known only to emigrants who return to their native land after a long absence. I soon find myself in a dreamy and wistful mood, apt to evoke long-forgotten experiences.

My life has not been especially eventful, a circumstance for which I ought to be thankful. Adversity and good fortune have come my way in the usual chance combinations of light and shade. The pains that seemed unbearable shrunk away, with time, to what I must deem their truer magnitude; likewise, events bright and fair lost their glimmer in the hazy distance. As I look back on this faint, dappled tableau, no different from the apportionment of most men, few patches seem still possessed of the original, vigorous luster. One episode, however, shines with a fantastic and unaccustomed light in the midst of the general dullness. It is my first encounter with the true image of death, whose silhouette thenceforth has seemed to me as if robed in an eerie glow.

I must have been nine years old. My third grade teacher announced, with a pleading accent and a plangent voice that conflicted with his usual stern, unsympathetic demeanor, that a child had passed away. "One of your peers," he said, "has ceased to

exist." I understood this to mean that a class-
mate had died; but since no one in my own
class had stopped attending school, I assumed that my teacher probably taught in
another shift, perhaps in another school, or
worked as a private tutor. The teacher's unusual address ended with an exhortation to
"pay our respects" to the deceased child and
his family. Those of us willing to do so were
to sign our names on a sheet by the classroom's door at recess. The school bus would
pick up the children who had signed on the
day of the ceremony, which was not a regular
school day. I was the first to sign up.

On the appointed day, clad in the
school's uniform—white shirt, gray trousers,
navy blue sweater with two horizontal red
bands across the left arm and the school's
embroidered emblem sewn on the front at
midchest—I waited for the bus at the usual
street corner holding my mother's hand. The
bus was late that day. I had expected to see
my classmates; none were there.

The bus followed an unaccustomed
route, since this time its destination was not
the school. I grew slightly apprehensive upon

realizing that I was the only passenger on
board. The prefect, or student monitor
(rather a menial entrusted with the undignifying charge of keeping a rowdy group of
children from relapsing into complete barbarism, but sometimes arrogating to himself
with sadistic relish the right to organize fights
into sportsmanlike boxing matches), was not
there, either. I was not frightened, however.
It takes stronger stimuli than those mentioned to move a carefree nine-year-old, who
is enjoying a school-sponsored outing on a
bright Sunday morning, in the direction of
fright. But I recall a certain feeling of uneas-
iness upon confirming the fact that no other
children were picked up during the long, cir-
cuitous course. The bus rolled deep into a
destitute area on the fringes of the city, where
dilapidated tenements, junkyards, and the
sparseness of people added a depressing note
of solitude to the unsettling experience.

The bus driver and I exchanged no
words. At last we arrived at our destination.
"It is here," he said, "follow the corridor."
We were in front of a multifamily dwelling
of the kind that were then called "*vecin-*

dades. " These were densely clustered hovels, often no more than a single room per family, with walls in wood or compressed cardboard and roofs of corrugated sheet metal. Often the tenants were squatters who had settled on an area lacking the most elementary sanitary services. Better established *vecindades*, such as the one we had come to, were made of densely aggregated habitations with winding passages or corridors between them leading to inner courtyards or "patios." In the latter stood fountains, or wells, or mere faucets. The precarious water supply, like the sanitary rooms, had to be shared. In the forties, *vecindades* could be found in Mexico City that could match, both in color and squalor, the most baroque descriptions of Eugène Sue's *Mysteries of Paris* in the nineteenth century. The patios followed one another along the labyrinthine corridors and were numerically identified according to their distance from the street. These dwellings, and the unique life experiences they fostered, became part of the local folklore. A popular song intoned the lamentation of unrequited love in the plaintive voice of a crooner: "Because I live in a fifth patio / You despise my kisses . . ."

I descended from the bus ready to obey the driver's instructions. I felt the childish worry that in an implausible fit of irresponsibility the driver might fancy that going back with a single passenger was not worth his while and abandon me there. To be alone and stranded in that squalid place was a disquieting idea. What followed was still more disconcerting: there was not a soul in sight. Fortunately, the corridor was short and straight, and I did not need to advance beyond the first patio. The direction that I was supposed to take was marked by mortuary crepes in white fabric, or ribbons tied in bows and suspended on the lintels and along the walls. I still had hopes of finding my teacher, or some of my classmates, in the room I was approaching. O, for the reassuring sight of a familiar face, even if it was that of a detested teacher!

I came at last to the designated place, a room facing the first patio. It was a mortuary chamber in whose center a child's coffin had been placed, supported on a stepping stool.

The lid was open. The corpse was that of a toddler who could not have been more than two or three years old. The room was bursting with odorous white flowers. Bouquets were densely arrayed everywhere: on the floor, at the base of the coffin's support, against the walls, lying on a table, placed within vases, or strewn in heaps upon the floor. It seemed plain that most of the room's furniture had been moved away in order to accommodate the masses of flowers. Upon entering the room, the observer's eyesight drowned itself in the thickly bunched profusion of bouquets, almost all white. And the dominance of this color enhanced the soft pastel blue of the child's coffin and the greenish complexion of the face it contained.

Awareness of death, a vivid realization of the caducity of life and its joys and miseries, constitutes the strongest drive for metaphysical interpretations. It is doubtful that any man would have ever philosophized without a consciousness of the immediacy and inevitability of death. At nine years of age one is far removed from any serious philosophical activity, but in no way impervious to the awareness of irrevocable death. When this awareness is realized, it is felt as a violent wrenching of our deepest being. Schopenhauer saw here the reason why the sudden sight of a human corpse always makes us solemn and grave.

There was no one in the room, apart from the lifeless body. No relatives, no mourners, no schoolteachers. Of the scenes that I had anticipated none came to pass. There were no rows of uniformed schoolchildren mounting guard by the coffin; no desolate parents shedding dolorous tears upon the untimely loss of their son. A dead child and I alone shared the silent enclosure. My anxiety grew from this realization, that both of us were as if enfolded in a common space, encased together in a compartment trenchantly divided from the world.

In a country where embalming and the art of "restoration" of cadavers is almost never practiced, the external appearance of my silent companion was not unexpectedly loathsome: his face was green and bloated. The unbearable stench of a cadaver in decomposition filled the room, mixed with the emanations of a thousand flowers. I understood that the room had been crammed with flowers in an effort to disguise the nauseating odor of advancing organic decomposition. I also realized that there is no quenching such a smell: pour the subtlest fragrances that human industry has devised, and you will obtain a juxtaposition of scents, not the predominance of the pleasant over the offensive. Bathe a decomposing cadaver in sweet perfumes, and it will smell of rotting carrion on a bed of roses.

The enervating, moldy, indescribable foulness revealed to me an unknown face of death. Until then, the visage of death had been a quiet, placid one, barely discernible from sleep. It was the face of historical personages laid out upon biers, surrounded by priests with crucifixes in their hands or relatives in mournful poses, as represented in book illustrations, lithographs, and paintings. It was also the image of obscure men who fall to the ground like broken mannequins in battle scenes of films: a fall that never wholly excludes from the mind of the spectator the possibility that the fallen will rise again in the next scene, like men who awake from sleep in their bedrooms. Now death was revealed to me in an altogether different guise. Not a passive and solemn form, but an actively vexatious one: a cadaver that offends; a dead body still capable of outrage and aggression; a clawing, screeching, rending thing that hurls disagreeable sights and unbearable smells. At the foot of the supporting stool was a glass jar containing some money, and I deposited in it the few coins that I carried.

I returned to the school bus that awaited me. The motor was still running. I must have stayed in the room for less than three minutes; to me, they were three centuries. I experienced a diffuse anguish, an inexpressible anxiety. To equate this feeling with merely being scared would be an unperceptive oversimplification. I was torn between the impulse to flee the place, running, and the sense of duty or the fear of appearing cowardly, which kept me there.

Who was that child? Why was his cadaver left unattended amidst a sea of flowers? Where were his parents, his grieving relatives, the neighbors, the children expected to participate in the funeral ceremony? Undoubtedly, a logical answer to these questions could have been supplied. None was ever revealed to me. When school resumed, the teacher made no mention of the occurrence; nor was he the type of mentor I should have wished to discuss the matter with. My closest friends had not signed up. No one else had attended. My parents knew nothing about my experience, and I would never have troubled them without weightier cause. The extraordinary circumstances surrounding this episode, like the complexity of the feelings it elicited in me, vastly surpassed my childish ability to articulate a coherent, rational interpretation of the affair. Therefore, I was forced to file it raw and unresolved in the archives of memory. Perhaps its only enduring consequence has been to make me see a very personal landscape in the legends and myths that talk about the netherworld. Heroes who, like Orpheus, descend to Hades, I imagine walking through threatening passageways in the semblance of the corridors and patios of an old Mexican *vecindad*.

Many years later, my profession was going to confront me—fortunately with extreme rarity—squarely with the spectacle of decomposing cadavers. For sooner or later, after the heart has ceased to beat, the body will decompose. It is, in fact, no longer a human body, but a corpse; and having acquired a new ontological category, it must join a dialectic to which it used to be alien, namely that interplay of contrasts in which human nature is opposed to inanimate object, cleanliness to filthiness, and permanence to decay.

No civilization has been able to face without horror the spectacle of a putrefying cadaver. The ascetics of India, who found it especially loathsome, summarized the corpse's three possible fates: to be eaten by predators, then turn to excrement; to be buried and turn to maggots; or to be cremated and turn to ashes. Needless to say, of the three they found the last one the least offensive way to recycle the body's constitutive elements. In Brahmanic thought, cremation is more than ecology-conscious disposal: it is also a sacrificial offering. Accordingly, the lame, disfigured, or deformed are not deemed worthy of the flames, and theoretically must be first immersed in the cleansing stream of the Ganges. It is the same for spiritual pollution: the sinful would contaminate the fire. Of a corrupt government official in Bihar, suspected of prevarication during life, it was said that his corpse refused to burn despite the liberal smearing of resins and the huge size of the pyre. Conversely, it is a folk belief in India that the faithful wife who self-immolates in her dead husband's pyre ignites spontaneously. Virtue as combustibility. I think of the lithograph hanging on the wall of my mother's bedroom, which represents the Sacred Heart of Jesus in the shape of a stylized, playing card's heart all aflame.

SCENE THE SECOND

During these depressing musings I have wandered into my old neighborhood. It is much changed, but it remains a working-class *barrio* teeming with children. Before I can negotiate entrance to my former apartment building, I must wait until the tactical offensive of the youngsters' soccer team playing in the street is repelled by the embattled defenses of the adversary team. Some things, I say to myself, remain much the same.

My mother and my uncle occupy the apartment. Both are in their eighties. She is the younger of the two; her brother borders closely on the ninth decade. I knock at the door and my mother receives me effusively. Although the difference in years is not very pronounced, the state of preservation of my mother and my uncle differs markedly. My uncle became a widower recently, and his bereavement hurt him deeply. I have been told that he has withered swiftly and all too visibly.

As soon as my mother and I sit to chat in the living room, he emerges dressed in his best finery, which he has donned, I believe, for the occasion of my visit. The jacket is clearly too big, and the wrinkled shirt is painfully discordant with the outmoded, shiny necktie. He is obviously conscious of his ill-fitting, threadbare attire, and over my protestations he begins to apologize: he has lost much weight recently and has not yet had a chance to renew his wardrobe. Rather untactfully, my mother declares: "He has plenty of good shirts. But he keeps them in a drawer and never wears them. Would you believe it? He says those were the last shirts that his late wife personally ironed for him, and he dares not unfold them."

My uncle is taken aback by the abrupt disclosure of this intimate detail, but does not seem upset. He looks genuinely moved at the mere evocation of the cause of his sartorial disarray. A sudden shadow grows over his face. Lowering his head, he mutters repeatedly: "A good woman . . . A wonderful woman . . . I tell you, a *good* woman . . ."

Decidedly, the man is an irredeemable romantic. At ninety, this ought to be reckoned no small handicap.

I find it difficult not to contrast past memory with present, objective percept. I remember him as a sanguine, vigorous man. Sentimental, he was not. Although of humble birth and very limited education, he made up with daring and resolve for what he lacked in the subtler means of worldly advancement.

Intense, brisk, trenchant, and possibly a bit too caustic for his own good, he fell in with the workers' movement. I mean those circles of proletariat advocacy in the old-fashioned sense; when one could without contradiction wave red flags, preach internationalism, salute the purity of Soviet Leninism, and keep a clear conscience and a straight face—all at the same time. But the stint worked out badly. One evening, after a rally, he was chased by armed henchmen on the company's pay—"scabs," as he called them —across the brewery's courtyard and into protracted unemployment.

This happened in the forties. At that time, labor contracts came easily to able-bodied Mexican males who did not mind easing hunger by leaving their country to support the booming postwar economy of the most powerful nation on earth. If emigration patterns are reliable indicators of the matter, acute conflicts between conscience and stomach are usually settled to the benefit of the latter. Accordingly, my uncle joined the hardy crews that picked the fruits born of the same soil that supported the bastions of soulless capitalism and imperialistic domination. As far as I could tell, the shock to his socialist conscience was without abiding ill effects.

For more than a decade the contracts were periodically renewed. My uncle picked cotton in Texas, tomatoes in California, potatoes in Iowa, oranges in California, and assorted produce as far north as Montana, Michigan, and Wisconsin. The bounty of the earth, difficult as it seemed to us to understand, still explodes with strawberries and varied fruits in the interval between icy crustings in those lands.

We saw him sporadically. Quite a ceremony it was, during his fleeting home visits, to see him unpack his hard-earned treasures: alarm clocks with dials that glowed in the dark, still with a Woolworth's label; thick jackets bought in army surplus stores; battery-operated shortwave radios; toothbrushes attractively packaged in plastic containers with transparent cellophane windows; and slick fashion magazines in glossy paper, redolent of fine ink, which featured tall, blond, blue-eyed beauties in swaggering poses. And after the unpacking, most dazzling of all, came his tales of labor activism. My mother and I would sit to listen to the accounts of his self-abnegation, and how by becoming the trusted man of the foreman he strove to redeem the sad lot of his illiterate and downtrodden brethren. The populist in him was not extinguished, and his enormous vitality continued to support him through the back-breaking, dawn-to-dusk work shifts, the evening rallies, the soapbox harangues, and the distribution of mimeographed sheets where his coworkers would glean, with great difficulty, the advent of a new era.

The harshness of a migrant worker's life, and the intensity of a labor organizer's, still left him time for a tumultuous series of amorous adventures. He had a total of six wives, on both sides of the border, reckoning common-law and duly certified ones; five of them he survived, four he irresponsibly abandoned. I thought him a strange mixture of Danton and Casanova; a portentous experiment of nature by which many life-affirming genes had fortuitously converged in a single individual. Only this volcanic man has now turned into a decrepit, pitiable being "sans eyes, sans teeth, sans everything" who tells me in a piping voice while pointing at his thin frame and sagging flesh: "Do you see me? I am only skin and bones, but I cannot finish dying."

In effect, time has operated its relentless erosion. This is the sense of the popular metaphor: death is ensconced in the body, lurks in the interior of the tissues, and by our progressive structural dissolution it becomes more and more apparent each day. As Plato proposed a suprasensible essence behind the surface of things in this world, so death would lie hidden somewhere behind the epidermis of this body. The skeleton, which is the symbol of death, reveals itself slowly; the bony prominences proclaim themselves to the exterior gradually tightening the skin. Death underlies life, and the action of time consists in peeling successive layers so as to render it ever more visible.

The layers that remain, those that are not yet degraded, become flabby and yield to the earth's gravitational pull. The story is told by Diogenes Laërtius of a Greek philosopher who in advanced old age tripped and fell to the ground. He pounded the earth with his fist while saying: "Why do you call me so rudely? I am coming, I am coming of my own accord." The earth tugs on us daily, hour after hour, year after year, until at last we succumb to the pull and she receives us in her lap. For my uncle, the effects of the prolonged gravitational pull are all too evident. I must conclude his definitive fall is imminent.

Struck by his startling announcement, I pretend not to understand, and he repeats: "Yes, all my friends and contemporaries are long dead. Me, I just can't finish dying." *No me acabo de morir:* "I cannot finish dying." The unusual sentence construction suggests to me that my uncle subscribes to the popular belief that life, or at least old age, is a continuous dying, since he professes not to be able to finish what implicitly he already started. When exactly do we begin dying? Perhaps at birth. But in that case the living state would be a long agony, or better yet, a series of partial destructions strewn along the road of individual existence and culminating in total destruction. I don't know what perverse inclination moves me to ask him: "Are you impatient? Would you rather finish?" Much to his credit, my callous impertinence does not alter his polite equanimity. Firmly, very firmly, but without any detectable resentment, he answers: "Of course not. Life is the most important thing we have."

This answer seems to confirm my suspicion that life is not a series of minideaths. If it were, the final death could hold no terrors for anyone. It would be one more trivial event in a series of cognate, trivial events. My uncle should then be unconcerned, since death might come as a routine happening. Deaths would be entirely without pathos. But, in truth, extreme old age is no half death: it is every bit as vital as the bloom of youth, only different. The tempo is slowed down, the tension has slackened, but the qualitative nature of being is the same: physiologically diminished, ontologically intact. When my uncle confesses that life is important, he declares himself a passenger aboard life's vessel, a believer in life's flow, in the direction of becoming. For only death annihilates all sense, all becoming, to replace them with non-sense and absolute cessation.

At the end of the conversation, my uncle has fallen deeply asleep in his armchair. I say good-bye to my mother, and ask her not to disturb him. I leave the apartment with that bitter pang that comes from not knowing when or *whether* I will see my loved ones again.

I fly back to Chicago the next day. On the plane, I think more insistently of the two scenes that the cameras did not record than of the many that were captured. Two scenes: one reminisced, one witnessed. That one of a child who feels for the first time the diffuse anguish of death; this one of an old man who experiences the supreme lassitude of life. The two weigh the same. Between the youth who yearns to run out of a funeral chamber and the senile man who anticipates his own funeral asleep in his armchair, the link is one of equivalence. Infinite hope with few regrets, or infinite regrets with little hope: the tally is the same. A long stretch of futurity ahead and a brief stream of preterit behind, or a huge trail of preterit and a thin rim of futurity: they are exactly the same worth. Only death, which has no hope, no regrets, no preterit, no futurity, no lassitude, no anxiety— only death outweighs them both.

Moonlight Autopsy

The film director asks me, point blank, for permission to film an autopsy. This request raises serious misgivings on my part. All sorts of people apply for admission as spectators to the morgue, a fact that I found initially quite surprising and not undeserving of detailed attention. The reiteration of the requests led me to question each time the legitimacy of the underlying motivation and to set strict standards for granting permission. These standards I am now asked to abrogate, since to film the autopsy for television is to bring its gory aspects straight "into the living rooms," as the saying goes, of a broad public. I am therefore compelled to canvass the criteria that separate scenes "viewable" from those that ought to remain concealed.

Any spectacle that includes the shedding of blood is potentially capable of triggering profound and uncontrollable reactions in the spectator. This seems self-evident and is supported by repeated experience. The effect may be so unsettling that the self becomes dislocated from its normal bearings: hence that extraordinary phenomenon, to this day incomprehensible and mysterious, that consists in swooning upon the sight of blood. It is as if the consciousness had a momentary intimation of its own destructibility, a flashing but incontrovertible realization of its own mortality: not a general, abstract knowledge that we are all mortal, but a concrete and immediate prescience that death is in each of us. It is as if the red and viscous fluid, gliding free, represented to the mind that our lives are rivers that stray to a sea of nothingness; and this terrible image is found so utterly unbearable that the brain prefers to blot it out, to cancel it altogether by suppressing all sensations and all perceptions in a single, abrupt drawing of curtains.

The film director assures me that all the members of his crew are seasoned, hardy veterans; that they have filmed various surgical operations; and that, in fact, autopsy scenes have been formerly aired on British television. But there are other reasons for my reluctance, quite apart from the unlikely possibility that a filmmaker might suffer a fainting episode in the autopsy suite. I am troubled at the prospect of projecting a false image of the pathologist as a specialist constantly immersed in a harrowing, gloomy ambience of evisceration and gory spray. At a time when the autopsy has become a declining and unpleasant task for most pathologists, undue emphasis on this part of an interesting and varied job would be false and unwelcome. Most of all, I worry that a depressing portrayal of the hospital in which I work might be beamed to the world, thereby undoing in five minutes years of assiduous toil by the dedicated staff of the hospital's public relations department.*

This brings me back to the question I was asked: What do I think of filming an autopsy for public viewing? In the context of

---

*Although the latter consideration is purely political, it is by no means negligible. Today, North American hospitals must be exquisitely sensitive to the way they are perceived by the communities they serve. Economic woes are at the origin of the hospitals' carking and caring, especially caring about their public image. Why, with the scandalous price of liability protection for medical doctors, the just claims from nurses for equitable wages after overlong discriminatory practices, and the massive investments of capital needed to implement modern medical advances, the hospitals are in great difficulty to comply with the peremptory demands that sophisticated medical care be available to all. For the escalation of the cost of medical care is happening at a time when the government, faced with a huge federal deficit and an unfavorable trading stance, decrees all sorts of measures to contain it. Therefore, the hospitals are unfortunately caught in the middle of two opposing and irresistible forces: those that drive the cost of medical care upward, and those designed to abate it.

A climate of fierce competition has developed. For-profit hospitals often capture financially solvent patients and patients with relatively benign diseases, while those unable to pay, or with poorest chances of survival, whose care is more expensive, are left to public hospitals or to specialized, "tertiary-care" institutions such as mine. In response to this frustrating situation, hospitals have restructured themselves in the image and semblance of large corporations, for which, as everybody knows, advertising and publicity are fundamental aspects of survival. Only a decade ago, advertising was still deemed undignifying or ethically suspect by the medical profession. Today, many hospitals reserve an impressive part of their budgets for this purpose. In 1984, a newspaper in Florida (*Miami News*, April 9) reported that ten major hospitals in that state were spending twenty times more in advertising compared to the amount spent for this activity only three years before.[1]

the aforesaid, I cannot stop pondering about its effect on public relations; and I suspect the public relations department would consider it as outright sabotage. For to film the autopsy is to film death's triumph and the hospital's ultimate failure. Death is an incontrovertible denial of the power of all the electronic gadgetry and the gleaming equipment and the organ transplants and the intensive-care units. It is a humbling denial of the helicopter transport system and the purposive, smiling, optimistic staff shown in expensive promotional advertisements. In the world of advertising, hospital patients never die: who would think of suggesting otherwise? Therefore, to allow visual documentation of the triumph of death is to place myself squarely outside the mainstream of institutional correctness. I have visions of opprobrium and disgrace; of being branded irresponsible and disloyal to the very organization that secures my livelihood. Not without some ambivalence at my own want of assertiveness, I remit my answer to the sanction of my superiors and the acquiescence of the P.R. department.

In the discussions that follow I am pleasantly surprised by the cooperativeness and good sense of the hospital authorities. Considering that the documentary is not intended to be a technical biomedical presentation and that its selected focus is the literary, not the scientific accomplishment of one of the members of the staff, the restrictions imposed are surprisingly few. Practical difficulties remain, however. Postmortem studies are on the decline, for many complex reasons amply discussed in the specialized literature. Weeks might elapse, I say to the film director, before a postmortem study is requested; and the cost of the film production cannot be maintained indefinitely. On the other hand, there may be more than one in a single day. We have no way of telling whether the days ahead will bring an absence or a surfeit of requests from the hospital staff. A member of the film crew is assigned the task of checking our schedule several times a day, and the team's activities are planned accordingly.

Not long thereafter, I receive notice in the evening that an autopsy is expected for the following day. When the members of the film team are gathered to plan their work, I cool their enthusiasm with a disturbing piece of news: the patient to be studied succumbed to acquired immunodeficiency syndrome (AIDS). Every member of the crew will have to observe detailed precautions and wear protective garments, including gloves, surgical masks with protective shields for the eyes, and head and shoe covers; furthermore, only the most indispensable crew members will be admitted to the autopsy room during the actual performance of the anatomical dissection. My serious admonitions visibly weaken the group's resolve. Nor do I think them exaggerated or unwarranted. Hazards exist in the autopsy suite, even in this era of potent antibiotics. No drug exists to kill the hepatitis virus; the virus that causes Creutzfeldt-Jakob disease, a rare form of progressive dementia, survives even after prolonged immersion of infected tissues in formalin; and tuberculosis may be acquired, to this day, upon exposure to the causative bacteria in the morgue.

The danger of contracting AIDS from participation in the autopsy of a patient who died of this disease is less well studied. To the questions of the worried moviemakers I merely answer that the risk is very low for those who will stand at some distance from the table dressed in full protective apparel, since they will not come in direct contact with blood or secretions. But there is a heightened concern about the risk of this dreadful affliction, which is known to all from reiterated media coverage. When the medical profession has been disturbed by requests from physicians who wished to be removed from the care of patients with AIDS out of dread of contagion, it is hardly surprising to find a high level of anxiety among the laity.[2] The cameraman would like to hear that the risk is nil, and my constant reiteration that it is very slight does little to allay his fears. The other members of the crew stolidly declare that they will do as he does; but this abdication of the collective responsibility for decision only adds to the perplexity of the photographer, already ill-disposed to embark on a job whose risks no one seems able to fathom precisely. After much circular talk, we come to no determination. The appointed decider needs some time to think the matter over. We part without knowing whether the filming will take place.

Very early the following morning, a telephone call informs me that the crew is ready. The cameraman's hesitations were undone; not by protracted soul-searching, but by the polled opinions of his physician friends, who assured him that the risk was of such magnitude as would not justify turning down the job, provided elementary precautions were followed. When I arrive at the autopsy suite, the lighting arrangements are complete. Instead of the usual fluorescent tubes on the ceiling, complete control of the illumination has been secured by expertly disposed powerful lamps resting on upright stands at critical sites. Undesirable noises have been suppressed by a number of measures, all to the benefit of the sound track. The hum of refrigerators and other equipment kept in the morgue is utterly silenced.

I have familiarized myself, as is usual, with the details of the deceased patient's clinical history. The subject is a boy, not yet nine years old, who acquired the disease from his drug-addicted mother: "vertical" transmission of the virus, across the placenta, is today the commonest route of infection in young children. Symptoms in those cases manifest in the first two or three years of life, or else the disease presents a more chronic course in which growth and development occur in parallel with the progressive devastation wrought by the disease, as happened in this case. A brief perusal of the clinical record unveils abysmal depths of human suffering couched in the impersonal, technical phraseology of clinical histories, always with a partiality for the passive form of sentence construction: "Because the patient's mother succumbed to the disease, it was decided to test all the family members at risk . . ." or "In view of the father's inability to care for his child, it was believed that the patient should become a ward of the state . . ." Who "felt" that everyone should be tested? Who "believed" that the unfortunate orphan should become a ward of the state? The clinical history simply does not say.

The proceedings are briefly interrupted when two clinicians come down to confer with us and to advise us on the lesions they suspect to be present and to which they would like us to pay especial attention. They are quite intrigued by the preparations that are taking place in the morgue, but before they have time to question us their electronic beepers have gone off, summoning them away with the familiar, insistent, stubborn, high-pitched calls.

All is ready. On the floor, lamps on stands; on the walls, reflecting screens. On the table, an angelic, blond presence, from whose eyelids and cheeks color has fled, leaving behind such a wanness that none more troubling can be imagined. Not long ago this was a child; now it is a corpse, overspread by the coldness and clamminess of corpses, yet still retaining something of the living human presence. The livid hue, the icy chilliness, and the sunken outline cannot undo the ineffable residuum of humanity that clings to the newly dead: this is why dissectors often place a surgical towel over the cadaver's face before beginning their task. The recently departed are already unsentient husks, but their corpses may still be honored or outraged, exalted or vilified, reverenced or debased. The epic Homeric heroes fallen in battle were anointed, that their corpses should shine with a refulgence apt to strike awe in the hearts of their compatriots and their enemies alike. Dressed in magnificent armor, laid out on splendid biers, they were exposed to the admiration of all before being consigned to the fire. Only thus could their memory be forever enshrined in the chants of the poets. In contrast, the corpse of a hated foe was left to rot in the fields, dispossessed of all dignity. Achilles tied the corpse of Hector to his chariot and dragged it in the mud, that by covering it with filth it should be prevented from gaining everlasting glory. Devoured by vultures, torn to pieces by wild beasts, then incorporated into the substance of savage animals, the newly dead were disbarred from all the attributes of humanity and thereby excluded from the annals of human heroism.

I approach, scalpel in hand. Swiftly, unhesitatingly, I trace the long incision that starts the autopsy: the Y-shaped incision known to pathologists the world over since the times of the great masters, Virchow and

Rokitansky. All the steps in the procedure are carried out in the traditional manner: the reflection of the skin flaps, the exposure of the rib cage, the removal of the chest plate, the exposure of the thoracic and abdominal viscera, the dissection of individual organs, the attentive canvassing of every structure, and the repeated sampling of tissues for bacteriologic culture and other specialized studies.

On the surface, this is an autopsy like any other. But the externals attending this procedure are so different that a peculiar sensation gradually seizes me. Save for the whirring of the camera, an unaccustomed, heavy silence prevails in the room. It is an oppressive, thick, almost palpable stillness, which serves as a background alternatively to the brief staccato of scissors or knives, then the low-toned adagio of the saw, and then the largo of the suction pipes. Moonlight sonata. For the light is lunar. There are no windows, and the clever arrangement of powerful white lamps and reflecting screens and shades has the effect of diffusing a silvery glare, a brightness such as a full moon might project upon a quiet lake on a cloudless evening. Surely, this effect must have been studiously calculated by the director and the lighting man, the illumination expert who, all things considered, has preferred to abscond before I appeared to trace the first incision.

The metaphor of moonlight shining on a quiet pond or lake seems ill suited to a scene of anatomical dissection, but I do not know how best to describe the strange, eerie, pearl-white glimmer that floods the ambience. When the containers with liquid nitrogen are opened to receive pieces of tissue that must be frozen instantaneously for special studies, a vapor escapes that draws capricious arabesques in the air, like volutes with mother-of-pearl fringes. Then it seems as if we are all immersed in a perceptible thin ether, or as if we move in a submarine landscape.

The effect of lighting on the mind has yet to be investigated fully. A whole gamut of emotions, an entire register of affective tones and sensations may be elicited by modifying the lights, and thus the colors of the existing decor. I am certainly not new to the autopsy suite, yet it seems to me that I watch the developments taking place here for the first time. An insistent question obtrudes itself repeatedly in my mind: What are we doing here? Ostensibly, we perform a technical procedure aiming to uncover pathologic diagnoses, some already suspected and some new. In the top university hospitals the autopsy is still expected to disclose, in about 8 percent of the cases, major diagnoses that were entirely unsuspected in spite of the most sophisticated medical investigations done during the patient's life. Thus the autopsy is central to institutional efforts to upgrade the quality of medical care and teaching. But is this all? All these manipulations, all these activities in and around a cadaver suggest something else. A rich allusiveness and something like a hidden symbolism appear to emerge, as if tapped from a hidden source, through the uncanny synergism of light and silence.

It is impossible to avert the thought that our busy and purposive manipulations move us into the realm of the sacred. If an alien, detached, and intelligent being from a remote past civilization—say, a cultured Greek philosopher or a polished Chinese minister of the Heavenly Emperor from an ancient dynasty—were to peek through the camera at this moment, he would conclude that a religious ceremony of the utmost solemnity was being performed. For the opening of a human body is tantamount to penetrating the world of the sacred. Philosophers have remarked that mapping out space and establishing boundaries is the first step in the process of sacralization. Thus, not all the ground is the same: there is profane turf, which is left to lie fallow, and hallowed ground, wherein the faithful are interred. Not all houses are the same: there are unholy dens and houses of worship. There are cities of indifferent religious value and centers of pilgrimage, like Mecca, Lourdes, or Santiago de Compostela. Mircea Eliade opposed sacred space to scientific space; geometry he saw as the epitome of profaneness, since in geometry all space has exactly the same value, and the figures that are traced in this space can be done and undone without the least compunction.[3] But if this is so, the interior of the human body is surely the epitome of the sacred, since it is never penetrated without fear, awe, or passion. The interior of the body houses the energy necessary for all vital activities, the mysterious spark that propels life's flow and animates its stubborn pulsations: the interior of the body is sacred space.

In surgery, as in the autopsy, this sacred space is abruptly violated. Paul Valéry described what takes place during this violation in an immortal speech to the College of French Surgeons.[4] His description further persuaded me that my imaginary observer would have to conclude that he watched a religious ceremony of the deepest hieratic mystery. He would see a group of people robed from head to toe in strange vestments, talking in whispers to each other, masked, gloved, and never leaving the place of their ministrations, or if they do, never entering it again without first subjecting themselves to elaborate purification rites. One of them advances with a determined air, a scalpel in his hand—surely, this must be the high priest—and splits open the marvel of the human body.

The metaphysical consequences of this

simple act I had appreciated thanks to Valéry. Its real-life correlate was now revealed to me in unaccustomed detail through the contrivances of filmmaking: the inner recesses of the abdomen, thorax, and cranium are suddenly set in continuity with the outer environment. Every recess of the sacred space, every *sanctum sanctorum* is unveiled; every tabernacle is turned over. The loops of bowel, until then blind snakes that crept in total darkness; the heart, until then mad nightingale beating itself against the barred walls of its dank dungeon; and the brain, undisturbed contemplator who preferred, as did Immanuel Kant, a lightless thinking room for his abstractions; all are brusquely enveloped by brilliant flashes of light, and the sound of voices, and the tinkling of stainless steel instruments, and the multifarious emanations of the outer air. Barriers have disappeared, and the realms of the sacred and the profane merge into one with all the momentum of a tidal wave.

After the autopsy is finished, and all ancillary details are taken care of, I join the crew for lunch in a nearby restaurant. There is a feeling of relief, mixed with the satisfaction of having completed what no doubt will be the most powerful sequences recorded. The tone is jovial, and the cameraman is not spared some pointed teasing over his initial reluctance to participate, an anxious diffidence that continued through the early phases of the work and found a vent in the reiteration of reassurance-seeking questions: "Am I all right here?" or "Is this distance safe?"

In the relaxed atmosphere, I am asked many questions about medical aspects of death. Is it true that some physiological functions persist after a person is declared legally dead? To the merriment of the group, I quote a well-known television comedian's joke: "For two days after death hairs and nails continue to grow, but phone calls sort of taper off." Am I afraid of my own death? The pearl of wisdom is now Woody Allen's: "No. I am not afraid of dying; I just wouldn't like to be there when it happens." But the truth is that I, like any other man, cannot truly answer any questions about life's end. The greatest minds have been at a notorious disadvantage in this regard; for death, annihilation's epitome, annihilates all it touches like a highly contagious patient. Much worse than the patient we have autopsied today, death disseminates destruction all around. It annihilates even the thinking consciousness that attempts to frame it in concepts. It is impossible for death to be the object of a thinking subject, since a thinking subject is always a living subject. Thus death must be the object of no subject at all, which is impossible. If the paradoxes of the Eleatics were like coiled snakes that bit their own tail in closing a circular loop, death is the loop of a scorpion's tail, which turns back to destroy the thinking subject that posits it.

Nevertheless, death excites an enormous curiosity. How could it be otherwise? From the beginning of time human beings have left this life to emigrate to the unknown, dark realm, without any one of them ever coming back to hand us a report on the beyond. Any form of report. Not a word about what awaits us! We are curious by nature, but by nature doomed never to know. Never. True, life is a mystery no less puzzling than death, but at least we live ensconced in the former, and we can form some illusion that we are finding out its secrets. We are installed within life and inured to its constraints; surely this renders its limitations much easier to bear. But we are boxed in one enigma and separated from another whose existence we know without being able to even see it. Where is this enigmatic realm to which we are to emigrate sooner or later, all of us? Is it above or below? I am reminded of one of my former professors, a Spanish refugee who had sought asylum in Mexico during the frightful social convulsion of the Spanish Civil War. Having expressed dissatisfaction at the prevailing academic milieu of his adopted country, a student asked him whether he considered emigrating again to a new environment more suitable to his talents and proclivities. "Move on again?" he replied. "I am tired of roaming north, south, east, and west. I am too old. All that is left for me is vertical emigration, which is the only form of emigration I shall undertake in the future."

"Vertical" emigration, with heaven above and hell below, is only a manner of speaking. Death's realm is neither above nor below, neither to the right nor to the left. It is here and nowhere, which is the riddle that we express by saying that it is "beyond." But the astounding fact is that the realm of the living adjoins it; and though neighboring it very closely, it is separated from it by a thick partition with an opaque opening, across which not the faintest sound, not the dimmest glimmer ever filters. If perchance one of us decides to peek his head across the postern, he is sucked in and gone for good. The opening is one-way and so constructed that a barrier falls immediately behind those who intrude in the "beyond." The barrier is hermetic and infallible, so that the intruder can never go back. Never: a mousetrap more perfect cannot be conceived.

My merry companions in the restaurant do not agree. They talk about the "death experiences" of returnees, that is, persons who claim to have visited the beyond and managed to come back. They report various experiences, usually pleasant: feelings of levitation, flashing colored lights, flying across tunnels, or having their entire life represented in their view, as if they watched it in a movie theater. And since the company belongs to filmic circles, the conversation promptly turns to a current commercial film, *Flatliners*, in which daring and, one might suppose, rashly unphilosophical medical students subject themselves to induced cardio-respiratory arrest in order to assuage their curiosity about the enigma of enigmas. I am familiar, through television interviews and the popular press, with the claims of some of the alleged returnees. I have not watched the mentioned film. I grant that the narratives are colorful and highly entertaining, but I would object, on philosophical grounds, to the validity of the premise implicit in those claims.

As so often happens, the wrong use of language has buttressed and perpetuated a gross misconception. We speak of "cardiopulmonary resuscitation," CPR in medical parlance, when we really mean "reactivation." The philosopher Vladimir Jankelevitch[5] was among the first to point out the difference: it is technically possible today to reactivate a heart that has stopped beating provided certain conditions be met, such as the timeliness of medical intervention, but it is impossible to resuscitate a dead person. Reactivation of temporarily suspended or deranged physiology is sufficient proof that death has not occurred, since what characterizes and defines death is precisely the irreversibility of functional loss. If an engine that stopped working restarts when we tap it, we do well to correct our initial judgment: the motor, after all, was not completely broken down, and it was through an error of discernment that we formed a wrong opinion. Just so, if a man whose heart has stopped beating and whose lungs have ceased breathing suddenly regains the normal state, we ought to conclude that that man was not dead, a conclusion all the more certain for being obtained *a posteriori*. Certainly, his restitution to normal physiology could have been due to modern medical technology expertly applied. As Jankelevitch puts it, such reactivation "resuscitates the living, and is therefore the opposite of resuscitation . . . To pretend to produce a miracle when one reanimates a being who is not dead, is this not trickery or charlatanism?"[6] No doubt that person came very close to dying, disturbingly close—to the very edge of the abyss . . . but without falling.

A more reasonable conclusion would be that an error of perspective misguided us; that we were led to believe that the threshold to the dark chamber beyond was placed somewhere other than where it really is. We thought that stoppage of the cardiac action—a supremely dramatic phenomenon—marked the position of the threshold. Perhaps the highly dramatic quality of the observed phenomenon was the cause of our wrong belief. At any rate, we were misinformed, and medical science now retraces the portal's bearings with greater accuracy. Still, the magnificent progress of medical science should not delude us into believing that there is no categorical difference between reactivating temporarily suspended physiology in the living and raising the dead from the grave.

A medical profession that complains about the "unrealistically high expectations" of the public should have been more careful in its choice of language. It is wonderful publicity—and great flattery—to talk about "resuscitation" when "reactivation" or "reanimation" might have sufficed. It is too late to withdraw an expression that has become regular medical terminology; but flawed terminology must not obscure thinking and should not be permitted to mislead us into believing that modern medicine has revolutionized the metaphysical concept of death. Reanimation is a superb technical feat, but it is entirely out of proportion to resuscitation, which is a portent not seen since the time of Lazarus. By the same token, the duration of our lives has a unique significance to us from our individual perspective, but it is a duration that bears no possible comparison to the fathomless expanse of the ocean of time.

The ocean of time: its overpowering tide shall engulf us all, and by its repeated washings erase our traces until there is absolutely no mark of our existence—monumental memorials notwithstanding. Make no mistake about that. Modern medicine has granted us a short reprieve and might well increase our longevity. But it has not granted us immortality and never will. Overt or implicit claims of the P.R. department notwithstanding.

Lights, Camera, Stillness! Death and the Visual Arts

The film director-producer announces that he has permission to visit the Office of the Chief Medical Examiner and to film some of the gloomy activities that take place there. The day of his visit is to coincide with an uncommon event. A large truck, of the kind used by moving companies, is expected to pick up the unclaimed bodies previously placed inside pinewood boxes and to transport them to a cemetery on the outskirts of the city. Here, after bulldozers excavate a large grave, a mass burial is to take place, along with a religious service performed by an unattended Catholic priest. The producer

and his crew are excited. They hope to capture scenes unusual, striking, and full of visually powerful details.

My presence is not required, and I decline the invitation to join the group on this
lugubrious excursion. Frankly, more than a
week's continuous attention to matters funereal is beginning to have a draining effect
on me. I fail to see how a mass burial is
related to my activities as a pathologist and
wonder whether the projected film footage
has anything to do with the documentary that
occupies us these days, or if it is reserved for
a grander, future project. The director does
not say. It does not escape me that, from the
standpoint of aesthetics, the depressing spectacle might have considerable merit. Artists
of the past produced splendid allegories of
death full of macabre motifs, such as the famous fresco known as the *Triumph of Death*,
meant to decorate the walls of the *Campo
Santo* or cemetery of Pisa, in Italy. Brueghel
the Elder produced another painting of the
same title with scenes of carnage in grandiose
scale. The apocalyptic visions of Hieronymus
Bosch are well known. A bulldozer-driven

mass burial might produce the cinemato-
graphic, contemporary equivalent of the
scenes portrayed by these wildly imaginative
painters. However, I am not a professional
filmmaker, and rather than brave the icy
gales of Lake Michigan on a winter morning,
I prefer to stay behind and ponder the prob-
lems of visual or filmic representation of the
abstract concept of death.

In principle, the problem of an artistic
approach to death seems insoluble. Art passes
for being a majestic, life-affirming human effort. We think of it as a barrier against the
idea of death. Moreover, works of art are
undertaken with the thought of permanence;
they are meant to exist "outside time." The
humblest artist, if sincere, hopes that his or
her works will perpetuate themselves and go
on living at least beyond the normal lifespan
of a few generations. Additionally, artists attempt to remove us from the cares and
stresses of daily life. By that strange psycho-
logical mechanism that the ancient Greeks
dignified with the name "catharsis," aesthetic enjoyment distances us from all that is
terrifying in the certain fact of our complete

annihilation. More often than not, the visitor to an art museum or a picture gallery comes out persuaded that the world is perpetually regulated by benevolent gods and fairies whose chief preoccupation is to spread luminous reflections, golden tincts, and rosy hues over all the objects of the universe. If perchance the whim overtakes them to create repugnant or squalid beings, these are fashioned without violence to some notions of composition and symmetry.

Consequently, works of art never instantiate the aesthetics of death. Works of art are rather the exclusion of death. For art truly to represent death, it would have to include death's reality as part and parcel of the work. Only in that case we would no longer classify the work as art. For instance, splendid religious ceremonies may be entitled to the status of art forms. But if part of the ceremony includes killing, its artistic nature vanishes: it assumes the quality of a sacrificial offering. If it includes a human sacrifice, the sacramental character—to say nothing of the moral or legal undertones—overwhelms all other aspects. The ceremony becomes, above all, a sacrificial offering, and to rank it as artistic would seem misplaced. There are romantic souls, like Chateaubriand, who confess having been attracted to Catholicism by the impressive beauty of its pomp and ritual. Yet only the hopelessly unperceptive would continue to confuse religious conviction with aesthetic dilettantism, or mysticism with a personal preference for Gothic architecture, Gregorian chants, and Renaissance painting. In today's world there is no ceremony that would admit the reality of death as a component while still claiming to be an art form. The only exception is the bullfight. To hear Spaniards defend it, one cannot doubt the seriousness of their claim; but this highly debatable proposition cannot be discussed here without straying too far away from our subject.

How do the visual arts, and cinematography among them, come to grips with the abstract concept of death? A traditional solution is reification: death is given a specific, recognizable shape. Most often death appears as a skeleton, and it is not difficult to see why. A collection of bared bones is the body reduced to its lowest common denominator. Whereas the living body manifests motion, expressivity, or at least reactivity to external stimuli, the skeleton strikes us as a body minus its moving, expressive, and reactive parts; it is the barest, most basic human outline: a residuum incapable of further degradation without losing the human form. Indeed, further decomposition leaves behind dust, ashes, and finally nothing. *Hic jacet pulvis, cinis et nihil*, "Here lies dust, ashes, and nothingness," is the inscription on the tomb slab of a former grandee of Spain, the cardinal Portocarrero, buried in the cathedral of Toledo. It is a moving reference to our transitoriness, but one that would be of little use to the plastic arts. Ashes and dispersed molecules seem too remote from the human condition, and in art only a closer correspondence may be expected to arouse aesthetic emotions.

On the other hand, the skeleton is only one of several possible reifications. In Jean Cocteau's 1950 film *Orpheus*, death is an attractive young woman (actress Maria Casarès). Her lethality is suggested by her wearing surgical gloves and displaying the accoutrements proper to a member of the health-care professions—details for which my medical colleagues have little reason to feel thankful to the famous French artist. In Ingmar Bergman's 1956 film *The Seventh Seal*, death is a man attired in a long, flowing, black robe. Although his white face inevitably evokes a death mask, there is nothing frightening or terrifying in his serene, regular features. The genial Swedish director sets the action of this film in the Middle Ages and skillfully exploits the rich death symbolism that this troubled era bequeathed to posterity. In particular, a medieval theme that generations of artists have repeatedly rediscovered, the dance of death, is forcefully set forth. In the film, a painter is shown who works on a pictorial rendering of this theme; and the film's last scene is, in fact, an enactment of the dance of death, or *danse macabre*. No discussion of the visual imagery of death would be complete without mention of this ancient topic. It would require many a ponderous volume to summarize the scholarly research bearing on the origins and interpretations of this artistic motif. But some of the major facts brook retelling here, and we will attempt to do this in what follows.[1]

In Paris, not far from the Halles Centrales, the place where, until recently, the city's central market stood, there is a small public garden popularly known as "Les Innocents." This name derives from the site on which the park was built, which happened to be the cemetery adjacent to the Church of the Holy Innocents. As is well known, for many centuries burial grounds belonged to the Church. Now, this particular cemetery ranked high in the public esteem. The mighty and the humble, the rich and the poor were buried here without distinction. The cemetery of the innocents was hallowed ground if ever a piece of turf was deserving of that epithet. Bishop Louis Beaumont de la Forrest, who could not be buried there, disposed in his last will that some sand and gravel from the Innocents be sprinkled upon his tomb; and it is said that the earth from this cemetery and even the gravestones, now and then, were taken away to be sold for a handsome price among the faithful.[2]

High walls interrupted by three main

gates completely enclosed the area. It was on
the south wall that a mural painting was
started in 1424 by an unknown artist. At that
time artists virtually never attained the ce-
lebrity that may touch a few of them today.
In the Middle Ages they were mere artisans
who lived in princely houses on an equal footing with the fool that entertained the masters.
Thus, the artist who decorated the south wall
remained anonymous, yet managed to produce a motif that haunted the imagination
of the Western world for centuries, namely,
the dance of death or *danse macabre.*

The mural was destroyed in 1699, under Louis XIV, whose propensities were not
known to include a respect for the traditions
of antiquity. Happily, before the production
was turned to rubble in the name of so-called
progress and good taste, the figures in the
mural were copied in woodcuts, and these
were reproduced in a book by the famous
printer Guyot Marchant in 1485. Scholars
still argue about the faithfulness of the reproductions, but it is generally agreed that
these are, if not identical to the mural's figures, at least pretty close to the original.

The mural represented a procession or

a dance. Living persons and skeletons participated in it. The former were given attributes to facilitate their recognition, such as a triple crown to the pope, and a sword-and-globe to the emperor. They were carefully arrayed in an order of precedence: the pope came first, followed by the cardinal, the bishop, and so on. All in all thirty different personages representing many walks of life were portrayed, including the exalted and the humble. Thus, one could see king, duke, sergeant-at-arms, physician, bourgeois, usurer, monk, cleric, astrologer, and others. Death, represented as a skeleton, accompanied each living being. Each living being and its respective discarnate companion were surmounted by an arcading, and groups of four figures were separated from the next four by a column that, being thin, did not interrupt the flow of the composition. All were advancing to the left; most of the living members went forth reluctantly, tugged along by the corresponding skeleton. Verses were inscribed beneath each figure, often terrible in their satirical allusiveness. "The fattest rot soonest," says the skeleton to the

bewildered, portly abbot. The squire, presumably heretofore a carefree playboy, utters
a laconic and movingly plaintive *"Adieu
dames."*

The intent was moralizing and allegor-
ical; the spirit, satirical and sometimes grue-
somely caustic. Death, in the form of a
skeleton, approaches the distraught victims,
who are eager for a postponement, and seems
to tell them: "Well, your hour has just struck.
Come and join the dance." And neither the
replete usurer's money bag nor all the splendor of the potentate's imposing raiment can
obtain the slightest deferment.

It is impossible to underestimate the
power of this painting when viewed in the
context of the social milieu from which it was
educed. A visitor wandering in the cemetery
of the Holy Innocents in the Middle Ages saw,
at the end of the churchyard, behind an iron
grill, the austere cell in which it was said that
a woman had chosen to be immured for forty
years. The visitor might then stroll toward
the galleries or charnel houses built around
the cemetery's walls under a sort of covered
walk that existed there. The charnel houses

were bursting with the heaped bones and skulls of the dead that had to be disinterred in order to make place for the newly dead, as was the custom in many fast-growing medieval cities. And after contemplating this gloomy spectacle, if the visitor chanced to come up to the churchyard, he might have been able to hear the fiery sermon of some renowned preacher. For instance, Friar Richard, a Franciscan, addressed a crowd of between five and six thousand people from an open-air pulpit here in the year 1429. With his back turned toward the south wall of the cemetery, he unburdened himself of such a load of fire-and-brimstone rhetoric, full of allusions to the end of the world and the imminent coming of the Antichrist, that his breathless audience was whipped to a high pitch of religious fervor and threw gaming tables, playing cards, wine jugs, and various instruments of worldly pleasure onto a huge pyre.

This description may prompt us to think that the *Dance of Death* was the product of an irredeemably gloomy and dark era. History speaks of famines, epidemics, savage feuds, superstitions, treasons and tortures, and the incredibly protracted barbarism of a war aptly known as the Hundred Years' War. However, this is only one side of the coin. People's capacity for joyous exultation must have been in those days at least as robust as their stolid forbearance of their unimaginable ills. We sense that they were as ready to cast their pleasure-procuring objects into the flames as they were prompt to relapse into imbibing, wenching, gaming, and dancing after the first boiling of their neurotic piety. The same ambivalence applies to the *Danse Macabre.* On the one hand, it was meant to edify and to infuse feelings of a dark asceticism; on the other, it had an ornamental purpose, to strike a note of color on the bare walls of the cemetery.

Somber contrition and boisterous mirth went hand in hand in medieval times, and the *Dance of Death* was a typical medieval product. Its origins are traced to the early Middle Ages, but not down to classical Greco-Roman antiquity. It never occurred to the ancient Greek and Roman artists to represent death as a skeleton. This may seem odd to us, who are so completely inured to this symbol that we readily identify a bottle's contents as poisonous when we see a skull and crossbones on its label, and if the symbol is affixed to a door, we automatically think of a mortal danger beyond the threshold. However, the efficacy and widespread acceptance of this symbol does not mean that it is natural, in the sense of being somehow embedded in our preconscious selves. This graphic reification of death, today nearly universal, started off as a European fashion that dates from the fifteenth and sixteenth centuries.

The German dramatist Gotthold E. Lessing (1729–1781), who was also a writer on philosophy and aesthetics, set down in a mercurially polemical essay that the ancient Greco-Roman artists represented death as a winged youth or geni holding a torch upside down, as if to extinguish it, and grasping a laurel wreath on which rests a butterfly.[3] On an ancient sarcophagus the winged youth holds the reversed torch against the breast of a corpse. Lessing contended that the posture of the youth's feet, crossed one in front of the other, was another feature of the symbol. In support, he quoted a passage from Pausanias's description of a sarcophagus in the temple of Juno at Elis, on which was represented a woman with a sleeping white boy on her right arm, and a black boy on her left arm, who also seemed to sleep. Presumably, these were the twin brothers, Sleep and Death, Hypnos and Thanatos. The quoted passage from Pausanias contains a statement that scholars rendered into Latin as *distortis utrinque pedibus,* and into French as *les pieds contrefaits,* that is, crooked or deformed feet. Lessing argued in favor of still another rendering: not crooked feet, but crossed feet, "the natural attitude of a sleeper when sleeping a healthful, quiet sleep." Lessing eruditely multiplied the examples that allegedly made feet crossing the standard posture of sleepers in ancient classical statuary. He did not spare animals, for he cited two antique marble lions at a Berlin museum, whose forepaws appear crossed while their heads rest upon them during sleep. Much hot air was exchanged in philological circles during Lessing's time, but the matter of feet crossing was not settled. Evidently, sleeping posture remains highly idiosyncratic, and I suppose it may be rather exuberant even among staid philologists.

What was clear from Lessing's scholarly toils was that the ancients did not represent death as a skeleton. To be sure, skeletons are to be seen in ancient monuments, but apparently they are no more and no less than skeletons, and in no way do they pretend to represent the abstract concept of death. More recently, Jean Pierre Vernant has elegantly discoursed on the ancient Greeks' reification of the concept of death.[4] Thanatos was, indeed, a winged male figure. But he did not embody the terrifying aspects of death. He appeared in the midst of battles in a guise that hardly distinguished him from the other combatants, except for the wings that protruded from his back. His charge was not to kill, but to receive the dead into the otherworld, the "beyond" to which they gained access through the funeral rites. Death as a frightful force, as the embodiment of unspeakable and unthinkable terror, was represented by two feminine figures, Gorgo and Ker. Both represent the radical otherness, the maleficient powers that descend upon human beings to drag them into the obscure realm where their fate decrees that they be lost forever. Despite his winged body, Thanatos is no angel: his heart is of steel, and he forgives no one. But Gorgo and Ker hold greater terror. Thanatos is closer to "death beautified," a life's termination that does not exclude the possibility of an afterlife sustained by the epic songs of the poets. Gorgo and Ker are purely negative, destructive forces; they are long-nailed, execrable personages whose thirst for blood is never quenched.

In our day, the visual arts present us with other reifications of death. In a popular film directed by Milos Forman in 1984, *Amadeus*, based on the life of Wolfgang Amadeus Mozart, death appears as a male messenger arrayed in a sober, imposing attire. The filmmaker made use of a well-known anecdote from the life of the musical genius. The story refers to the musician's last days when his working schedule was so demanding, and his efforts so exhausting, that it passes for truth that overwork contributed to his death: in the middle of his tasks he suffered from fainting spells, so that his wife and attendants had to transport him to his bed.

Grueling schedules and frantic sprints to meet impossible deadlines were nothing new to this man. He once submitted with such haste the score of a concerto to be played at court that he did not have time to write down the part he was supposed to play himself. An exalted personage, puzzled at the blank score that the musician pretended to follow, asked him where his music was. "There!" replied Mozart, pointing at his own forehead. The overture to *Don Giovanni*, which many experts deem his best, was composed under similar self-torturing conditions. The entire opera was finished and was to be performed the next day, but the composer had not written a single note of the overture. Consequently, he had to work through the night. It is said that he asked his wife, Constanze Weber, to stay with him in order to keep him awake. She kept him company and told him stories that sometimes convulsed him with laughter, but fatigue would overcome him very soon after his wife fell silent. When she saw him fast asleep she allowed him to repose for a couple of hours, then woke him up again. In a mad rush he finished the overture just in time for the impresario and the conductor to pick up the score, while the ink was still fresh. On opening night, the overture of *Don Giovanni* was performed by musicians who had previously rehearsed the entire opera except the overture, which they were seeing for the first time. Stendhal stated that snobbish musicologists boasted that they could recognize which passages had been written by a sleepy composer and which ones had been composed when Mozart was startled into wakefulness.[5]

It was in this state of overwork, stress, and nervous exasperation that Mozart composed *The Magic Flute* and *La Clemenza di Tito*. One day, he heard a horse-drawn carriage stopping before his house. A man dressed in black, of mature age and imposing presence, asked to see the composer. Taken to him, the man declared that he represented a very important nobleman who had just suffered bereavement in the family, and wished to perpetuate the memory of the departed with a musical composition, a requiem. The messenger would not disclose the identity of his master. Mozart accepted the commission and set a price. The messenger disbursed the sum, unquestioningly and on the spot. It was agreed that the finished composition would be delivered in four weeks.

The composer set to work with even greater intensity than before. His health visibly deteriorated, and his wife and friends were alarmed. The requiem and the composer's health seemed to be linked in a sort of inverse proportion: the former grew as the latter withered. Mozart, like other men of acute sensibility, developed a neurotic obsession centered on his own death. "I compose the requiem for myself," he said; and he became persuaded that this work would be his last, and that its completion would sound the hour of his death. Moreover, he suspected that the messenger who brought the commission was not an ordinary human being, but a supernatural creature or a being with occult powers.

When the four weeks had passed, the messenger reappeared as mysteriously as before. Mozart was terrified: the work was not

finished. He stammered excuses and pro-
tested that he would finish the composition
in four more weeks. Ceremonious and polite
as usual, the messenger granted the extension
and left another important sum of money:
his master, he said, wished by this munifi-
cence to express his respect and admiration
for the greatest living musical genius. Four
weeks later, the requiem was completed, and
Mozart was no more.

Without resorting to the rather crude
technique of reification, as used in *Amadeus*
and other films, the visual arts may manage
to create a mental climate compatible with
the contemplation of the stark reality of
death. Funereal imagery is more effective in
the countryside, away from the productions
of human industry, which are often raised as
dikes against the idea of death. An obtrusive
architectural landscape will not do. If there
must be a human habitation, let it be a
ruinous castle with vines clinging to the win-
dowless, moldering walls; or a dark and oppressive enclosure such as would remind us
of the doorless house that shall be made ready
for us all, without exception, in the lap of the

earth. All things must be drained of too lively a power of suggestion. A quiet, immobile presence replaces the alarm, tumult, and struggle that are consubstantial to life. Think of subdued light coming down from a cloudy sky. Visualize a clearing in the meadows, softly shadowed by tall cypresses white with dust. All around, let there be tall oaks waving their fretted summits. And when the clouds rift asunder, and some light beams filter through, the leafless branches must trace gnarled, capricious figures on the ground: such are some of the trappings of the lugubrious, mood-setting landscape.

The approach of death is associated with a cold wind: this is a theme that recurs in poetry and legend since ancient times. Accordingly, cinematography fashions specters in white gowns agitated by the wind, or sea waves whose white caps explode against the rocks, impelled by a bleak and wild wind. American horror movies are justly renowned the world over for the mastery of such scenic effects. It is true that these films are, for the most part, abysmally inane. But only the most blasé can claim to remain untouched by the powerful imagery often shown. The images are skillfully drawn from the common fund of ancestral fears and ideas that Jung termed "archetypes" and symbols that slumber in the depth of our psyche. The atmosphere is dim and dark, but also cold and dreary. In this ambience, otherworldly beings stand immobile in the frosty air, their cheeks wan and withered, their garments waving in the wind.

The icy gales may thrust open a door or a window—another death-associated, primeval symbol—swelling the curtains. Or the wind may distend the sails of a ship that skims the horizon, as in the opening scenes of the vampire-haunted film *Nosferatu*. Cold, blowing winds, doors that open mysteriously, obscure personages that appear unexpectedly: these are forceful images. Unfortunately, most often they are placed at the service of cheap sensationalism or shocking gruesomeness. Only rarely does film succeed in being more than a diversion, or a trivial way to reinforce denial, and becomes something that we dare call art: a force able to lighten the weight of the existential anguish

that crushes us into dumb despair. Only
rarely do the visual arts succeed in lifting us
to the high pinnacle of aesthetic contemplation, whence it is possible to canvass our life's
end without anxiety.

In the lugubrious environment we may
come upon a figure in the twilight air,
whose features we cannot discern. This is
another death-conjuring symbol. A human
form whose identity escapes us places us in
front of the equivocal; confronts us with an
object bearing innumerable possible meanings. This effect may be achieved without
using veils or masks. In a film produced
during the seventies, *Death in Venice*, based
on a novella by Thomas Mann, a pitiable,
lonely, middle-aged man develops an ambiguous and irresistible attraction for an
androgynous-looking, delicate male adolescent. The action takes place in a seaside resort. In the final scene, the man dies while
watching the object of his adoration bathe in
the sea. His agony's pathos is enhanced by
this last vision of his love object placed
athwart the sun's radiance and aureolated
by a resplendent glimmer. Ordinarily, the
expected effect of strong illumination is to

reveal the identity of an object, but the place-
ment of a strong light source directly behind
it hides its features instead of revealing them
to the viewer. Is the adolescent thus seen a
human being, or is he the Angel of Death
crowned with a wreath of asphodel? From
the dying man's position, which is that of the
spectator, it is impossible to tell. All that can
be seen is a human figure, neatly delineated
by strongly drawn contours, but whose features are blackened by shadow, even as an
aura of intense light seems to emanate from
it like a creative force.

The artistic elements that can evoke a
mortuary mental climate have been the subject of study. Michel Guiomar is among the
scholars who have explored these elements.[6]
The effect of viewing a shadowed figure
against an intense light Guiomar calls *à
contre jour;* conversely, a brightly illumi-
nated figure against a shadowy background
is *à contre nuit.* In either case, the extreme
dynamic tensions that result from the interplay of lights and shadows foster an attitude
in the viewer that is especially favorable to
the presentation of funereal motifs.

It may be asked whether the aesthetic

preoccupations of scholars who research the artistic approach to death are relevant to our understanding of this momentous occurrence or merely idle pastimes. For art seems to run counter to our contemporary scientific and technological orientation. What we value most highly is accuracy, predictability, and rational interpretation. We tend to see death as a biological phenomenon and nothing more. But art dwells on the unintelligibility of death and underscores the vagueness of its boundaries. Not uncommonly, the scientifically minded condemn all appeals to the irrational or the portentous, in which art seems to find inexhaustible fountainheads for its creations. Why bother with myths and legends when the workings of a single cell are themselves a miracle that ought to compel our most reverent admiration? On the other hand, we detect a certain ambivalence behind formulations that speak of biological phenomena as "miraculous." We sense that this is only a manner of speaking, since it appears that science posits the body and its functions as subject to complete understanding: if not today, in a more or less distant future the workings of the body shall be thoroughly and accurately understood. However intricate and baffling its complexity might seem, the body is still *fabrica*, a cleverly assembled machine that can be made intelligible and therefore depleted of all mystery.

Jean Baudrillard has warned eloquently against the dangers of reducing the body to "the system of representations of a machine and its function."[7] Either a machine works, or it is broken down and does not work. Likewise, a living being is a machine in working order; a dead being is a broken-down machine that does not work. This thoroughgoing materialism trivializes death: a broken-down machine may pose a problem or a puzzle, but it holds no mysteries. Perhaps here lies the greatest danger, namely, that our thirst for myths is left unassuaged. Perhaps we hurt in our souls—if I may be forgiven the use of this archaic word—from chronic myth-symbol deprivation, just as the seafaring men of the past hurt in their bones from chronic deprivation of vitamin C. The sad consequences of this may be illustrated by comparing the significance of death in industrialized societies, where myths are held in contempt, and in communities alive to myths, symbols, and the influences of the imagination. In the former, someone who dies is, as Baudrillard puts it, *"quelqu'un qui fout le camp,"* that is, somebody who "scrams" or "takes off"—and that is all. It is an event without significance for the community. The dying die anonymously—the young never witness a death—and almost always in a hospital. In societies that we unabashedly call "backwards," death is a momentous occurrence with impact on the entire group, which solemnizes it with rituals and public ceremonies. An individual death is never trivial since it splits open the treasury of myths and symbols of the community.

If the dying are elderly, the differences are more pronounced, even grotesque. Among "backwards" people, the elderly enjoy a high social status: they are the keepers of the group's traditions, transmitters of knowledge, and dispensers of valued counsel. Accordingly, they die surrounded with the young gathered around the mortuary bed, eager to learn the lessons of those about to depart. In "advanced" societies the dying elderly have no words of wisdom. Not only because they cannot speak while tubes and monitors and intravenous infusions are upon them—what Baudrillard has called "technological last rites"—but because there is nobody to listen. And there is nobody to listen because their wisdom is called into question. The value of past experience is highly questionable in a world where more and more things are changing faster and faster. The accelerating speed of change renders past experience unreliable: the lived experience appears to be useless to cope with what is to come. The world therefore turns alien for all, but especially for the elderly, who have the greatest difficulty in keeping up with the struggle for renewal of rapidly obsolescent knowledge. One must be a lifelong student, says a noble maxim. True, but white-haired oldsters in the classroom, reduced to a plane of perfect equality with the immature and inexperienced, cannot inspire the young with the desire to flock to their elders for advice and guidance.

Art tends to counteract these ills by re-

vealing the multidimensionality of death. Art
uncovers the symbolic richness and the awesome, unfathomable mysteries that surround
life's end. Certain films, such as Ingmar Bergman's *Wild Strawberries*, have attempted to
restore to death its mystery and its dignity,
the two rightful dues that modern society
stubbornly denies it. In Bergman's film an
elderly physician (Dr. Borg, played by the
actor Victor Sjöström, who was also a director) sees his entire life condensed in a single
day. In the opening scenes the protagonist
dreams of his own death. He sees himself by
the roadside, in the woods. It is in the nature
of dreams, as of death prefigurations, that we
"clone" ourselves. We must create our own
"double" when thinking about our life's end,
for it is impossible to witness our own death,
even in imagination, unless it be by doubling
ourselves into one who dies and one who wit-
nesses. Many of the death-conjuring techniques of the visual arts are employed. In
his dream, Dr. Borg stands near a cradle,
and is shown *à contre jour*; the cradle is his
own, linking birth and death in an image
that mingles death's shrouds and an infant's

linen, softly agitated by the wind. He sees his
parents, separated from him by a span of
water, on "the other bank." But he remains
an old man.

Not much happens in the film, which
impresses us as the slow winding down of a
life's journey. The original Swedish title,
Smulstronstället, "The End of the Trip,"
seems much more apposite. In the opening
sequences the old man sleeps. It is a fore-
shadowing of death: in the plastic arts, as
in real life, the image of the sleeper is difficult to distinguish from the corpse. Short
of portraying cadaveric lividities or marks
of decomposition, a painter must face the
impossibility of depicting a deeper loose-
jointedness, a profounder unconsciousness,
than those annexed to sleep. In many a famous painting, a dead Christ proclaims his
death not through bodily posture, but through
the expression of unbearable suffering in the
Virgin Mary and Magdalene and the others
who lament the tragedy. In Bergman's film,
the last scene shows us again the main protagonist asleep, this time in a deeper slumber.
We become aware of the truth in a French

poet's statement, that *"Dormir, c'est essayer la mort"*: "to sleep is to 'try on' death."

Art is uniquely efficacious in stirring the wonderment and respect that are the dues we owe to death. Only art reveals its awesome import and gives us a hint of its multifarious, seemingly contradictory meanings. For it is by appealing to the emotions that we can aspire to a flash of intuition, very different from rational understanding, about a phenomenon that is at one time departure and arrival, farewell and welcome, abdication and crowning, annihilation and germination, end and beginning. Superior art does not romanticize death, nor does it condemn it as a hideous degradation. Neither does it set forth the banalization implied in the simile of the machine that does not work. All it does is set a certain tempo and create a certain climate: the former compels our hearts to beat in synchrony with the recurrent rhythms of nature; the latter makes us feel like the human plants we are, which grow and bloom in due season and are then felled by a wintry gush of wind unto the bosom of our mother, the earth.

Notes

A VISIT TO THE EMBALMER

1. Edward Johnson and Melissa Johnson: "Doctor Pedro Ara," *American Funeral Director*, Vol. 109 no. 4 (April 1986), 22–24, 60–62; Vol. 109 no. 5 (May 1986), 22–24, 76–78.
2. François-Marie Arouet Voltaire, *Letters on England*, trans. Leonard Tancock, Letter 25. On the *Pensées* of Pascal (No. 46) (Harmondsworth, Middlesex: Penguin Books, Ltd., 1980), 141.

THE GRIN OF THE *CALAVERA*

1. One of the best introductory works on the ancient civilization of the Aztecs is still Jacques Soustelle's *The Daily Life of the Aztecs*, trans. Patrick

O'Brian (Stanford: Stanford University Press, 1970). First published as *La Vie Quotidienne des Aztèques a la Veille de la Conquête Espagnole* (Paris: Hachette, 1955).

2. Alfonso Caso, *El Pueblo de Sol*, 7th ed. (Mexico: Fondo de Cultura Económica, colección popular no. 194, 1987).

3. Albrecht Dürer, "Tagebuch der Reise in die Niederlande, Anno 1520," in *Albrecht Dürer in seinen Briefen und Tagebüchern*, ed. Dr. Ulrich Peters (Frankfurt-am-Main: Moritz Diesterweg, 1925), 24–25.

4. Jacques Soustelle, *loc. cit.*, like all historians who dealt extensively with the ancient Aztec civilization, provides a comprehensive description of sacrificial practices. For a fanciful interpretation of the meaning of human sacrifice among the Aztecs, see Christian Duverger, *La Fleur Létale* (Paris: Editions du Seuil, 1979). Additional information is to be found in Louis Captian, "Les sacrifices humains et l'anthropophagie rituelle chez les anciens Méxicains," *Journal de la Societé des Américanistes* (Paris), Vol. 12 (1920), 212.

5. Octavio Paz: "Diosa, demonia, obra maestra," in *Los Privilegios de la Vista, Arte de México*, 1. *Arte Antiguo y Moderno*, 2d ed. (Mexico: Fondo de Cultura Económica, 1989), 39–58.

6. Justino Fernandez, *Coatlicue: Estética del Arte Indígena Antiguo*, 2d ed. Prologue by Samuel Ramos. (Mexico: Universidad Nacional Autónoma de Mexico, Instituto de Investigaciones Estéticas, 1959).

7. Octavio Paz, *loc. cit.*, 51.
8. Miguel León-Portilla, *Los Antiguos Mexicanos, A Través De Sus Crónicas y Cantares*, 8th ed. (Mexico: Fondo de Cultura Económica, colección popular no. 88, 1987), 121–122.
9. Paul Westheim, *La Calavera*, 3d ed., Spanish translation by Mariana Frenk (Mexico: Fondo de Cultura Económica, Breviarios del Fondo de Cultura Económica, no. 351, 1983).
10. Juan M. Lope-Blanch, *Vocabulario Mexicano Relativo a la Muerte* (Mexico: Dirección General de Publicaciones, Publicación del Centro de Estudios Literarios no. 10, 1963).
11. José Vasconcelos recounts this dark anecdote, apparently based on historical fact, in his novel *La Tormenta* ("The Storm"). Quoted in Edmundo Valades's anthology *El Libro de la Imaginacion*, 4th ed. (Mexico: Fondo de Cultura Económica, colección popular no. 152, 1987), 166.

OF SKULLS IN A HEAP
AND SOFT PARTS IN GLASS JARS

1. The funeral customs among the peasant population of the town of Mizquic have been studied by anthropologists and sociologists. One such study, containing recorded speeches by native inhabitants of this town is *La Muerte y los Muertos*, by Jesus A. Ochoa-Zazueta (Mexico: Secretaría de Educación Pública, Sep/Setentas, Vol. 153, 1974).
2. Quoted by Françoise Duvignaud in *Le Corps de*

l'Effroi (Paris: Le Sycomore, 1981). Translated into Spanish by Marcos Lara as *El Cuerpo del Horror*, (Mexico: Fondo de Cultura Económica colección popular no. 280, 1987), 102.

3. Charles Singer, ed., *Studies in the History and Method of Science*, Vol. 2 (Oxford: Clarendon Press, 1921). This work details the researches of the early anatomists, their methods, and their preoccupation with the preservation of specimens. Ruysch's exploits in the art of mummification of cadavers, which so greatly impressed Peter the Great, are described in a chapter entitled "The History of Anatomical Injections," by F. J. Cole, p. 307.

4. A photograph of the mentioned specimen, by Rosamond W. Purcell, accompanies my essay entitled "Anatomy and Old Lace," *The Sciences*, Magazine of the New York Academy of Sciences (January/February 1988), 48–49.

5. The excesses incurred by physicians of yore in trying to procure cadavers for dissection have given rise to a large body of literature. For a review of the vicissitudes of John Hunter and other British physicians of the eighteenth and nineteenth centuries, I consulted James Moores Ball, *The Body Snatchers* (New York: Dorset Press, 1989).

6. Isaac Disraeli: "Relics of Saints" in *Curiosities of Literature*, Vol. 1 (New York: W. J. Widdleton, Publishers, 1875), 323–328.

MOONLIGHT AUTOPSY

1. The sensible idea of hiring a philosopher-in-residence as part of the hospital staff was recently put into practice by a progressive-minded administrator of a hospital in New York City. The result of this interesting experience was a book that contains stimulating perceptions and fresh insights on the ethical dilemmas confronted during medical practice in a tertiary-care health center: *Drawing the Line. Life, Death, and Ethical Choices in an American Hospital,* by Samuel Gorovitz (New York: Oxford University Press, 1991). Advertising is an ethical dilemma, even though devoid of the drama of the life-and-death quandaries daily encountered inside hospital wards. The philosopher, Gorovitz, argued persuasively against the often alleged propriety of promotional advertising by hospitals.

2. The Council on Ethical and Judicial Affairs of the American Medical Association, upon hearing of the refusal of some physicians to treat patients afflicted with AIDS, issued a statement on December 1986 allowing that "not everyone is emotionally able to care for patients with AIDS . . ." and that those unable to do so ". . . should be removed from the case. Alternative arrangements must be made for the care of the patient." This statement was contrary to the self-abnegating tradition that has characterized the medical profession, and contradicts the position of clear unselfishness and altruism that was adopted from the outset by the Nursing Association. A new

statement was issued in 1987, a year later, which unambiguously declared that the primary duty of all physicians is to care for the sick, and that the dreadful nature of a diagnosis cannot be used as grounds for evading this fundamental responsibility. See Benjamin Freedman, "Health professions, codes, and the right to refuse to treat HIV-infectious patients," *Hasting Center Report* (April/May 1988), 20–25.

3. The "sacralization" of space in the historical evolution of a religious mentality is discussed, with the usual wonderful erudition, by Mircea Eliade in his book *The Sacred and the Profane*, trans. Willard R. Trask (New York: Harper Torchbooks, 1961).

4. Paul Valéry, "Discours aux chirurgiens," in *Oeuvres*, Vol. 1 (Paris: Gallimard, Bibliothèque de la Pleiade no. 127, 1957), 907–923.

5. Vladimir Jankelevitch, *La Mort* (Paris: Flammarion, 1966).

6. *Ibid.*, 310.

LIGHTS, CAMERA, STILLNESS!
DEATH AND THE VISUAL ARTS

1. My main source of information on the *danse macabre* was the admirable scholarly monograph by James M. Clark, *The Dance of Death in the Middle Ages and the Renaissance* (Glasgow: Jackson, Son & Co., 1950). It is reproduced in *Death and the Visual Arts* (New York: Arno Press, Literature of Death and Dying series, 1977). See also

Alfred Scott Warthin, *The Physician of the Dance of Death* (New York: Arno Press, 1931).

2. *The Cemetery of the Innocents and Its Charnel House, Paris, during the Reign of Francis I* is the title of a painting of the Flemish school that portrays *Les Innocents* in its pristine state, during the sixteenth century. The painting is part of the collection of the Musée Carnavalet of Paris, and is reproduced in a book by Philippe Ariès, *Western Attitudes Toward Death: From the Middle Ages to the Present*, trans. Patricia M. Ranum (Baltimore: Johns Hopkins University Press, 1974).

3. The monograph by Gotthold E. Lessing, "How the Ancients Represented Death," is reproduced in *Death and the Visual Arts.*

4. Jean Pierre Vernant, "Figures féminines de la mort en Grèce" in *L'Individu, La Mort, L'Amour: Soi-même et l'Autre en Grèce Ancienne* (Paris: Gallimard, 1989).

5. Marie-Henri Beyle (Stendhal), "Vie de Mozart" in *Vies de Haydn, de Mozart et de Metastase, Oeuvres completes de Stendhal,* Vol. 41 (Geneva: Edito-Service, S.A., 1970), 293.

6. Michel Guiomar, *Principes d'une Esthétique de la Mort* (Paris: José Corti, 1967).

7. Jean Baudrillard, *L'Echange Symbolique et la Mort* (Paris: Gallimard, 1976), 249–254.